LIVING THEORY

LIVING THEORY

The Application of Classical Social Theory to Contemporary Life

CHARLES E. HURST

The College of Wooster

ALLYN AND BACON

Boston ■ London ■ Toronto ■ Sydney ■ Tokyo ■ Singapore

Series Editor: *Sarah L. Kelbaugh*
Editor in Chief, Social Sciences: *Karen Hanson*
Editorial Assistant: *Jennifer DiDomenico*
Marketing Manager: *Brooke Stoner*
Editorial-Production Administrator: *Annette Joseph*
Editorial-Production Service/Electronic Composition: *TKM Productions*
Composition Buyer: *Linda Cox*
Manufacturing Buyer: *Julie McNeill*
Cover Designer: *Jenny Hart*

Between the time Website information is gathered and then published, it is not unusual for
some sites to have closed. Also, the transcription of URLs can result in unintended
typographical errors. The publisher would appreciate notification where these occur so that
they may be corrected in subsequent editions. Thank you.

Library of Congress Cataloging-in-Publication Data

Hurst, Charles E.
    Living theory : the application of classical social theory to
contemporary life / Charles E. Hurst.
      p.   cm.
    Includes bibliographical references (p.) .
    ISBN 0-205-27775-6
    1. Social sciences--Philosophy. 2. Marx, Karl, 1818-1883.
3. Durkheim, Emile, 1858-1917. 4. Simmel, Georg, 1858-1918.
5. Weber, Max, 1864-1920. I. Title.
H61.H93   1999
300' .1--dc21   99-19228
                                      CIP

Printed in the United States of America

10 9 8 7 6 5   04 03

To Katie, Brendan, and Sarah:
All different, all wonderful, and all loved

CONTENTS

CHAPTER THREE
Private Lives and Public Connections   41

CHAPTER FOUR
Separatism and Status   59

CHAPTER FIVE
The Decline of Civility: Cynicism, Corruption, and Other Nastiness   79

CHAPTER SIX

**Commodification and the Value
of Human Life   99**

CHAPTER SEVEN

The Polarization of Economic Resources   123

PREFACE

■ ■ ■ ■ ■

Trying to make almost 100-year-old social theories come to life and demonstrating their usefulness in contemporary society is a difficult task in itself. Trying to make them come alive for undergraduates is even more daunting, but necessary if we are to make students realize the enduring value of classical works. I have taught courses in social theory for almost 30 years, and during that time I have come to recognize how much students appreciate being shown how theoretical ideas apply to issues and topics with which they are familiar. Applying classical social theories to current subjects draws students into a deeper discussion and understanding of theories, both their strengths and their limitations.

While I recognize that the work of classical theorists has been interpreted, reinterpreted, and updated in contemporary theories, I believe that classical theories in their original forms still have much to teach us about social life. One of the principal reasons they are called *classical* is that the issues they address recur in modern societies, such as in the United States. I have chosen Karl Marx, Emile Durkheim, Georg Simmel, and Max Weber as classical representatives because of their continuing influence on contemporary social theory and because they addressed many of the central issues we confront today in modern society. Certainly there are limitations to classical theories as analyses of contemporary society, and, on a number of occasions, I point these out in discussions of social issues. But the considerable strengths of classical social theories warrant their usage in understanding issues and trends in today's society.

Consequently, this book presents much of the core content of classical social theories, but its focus is on the application of theoretical arguments to several issues involving social distance and separation in the United States. I emphasize the theme of social distance and separation because so many discussions of current social problems—such as alienation, segregation, and political apathy—concern questions of social distance, separation, and disunity. Given that the United States is a large, structurally complex, socioculturally heterogeneous, and changing society, it should not be surprising that a focus would be placed on concerns of social distance and unity. I wish to emphasize, however, that social distance and separation are not always negative forces in society. The confrontation between the individual and society, and the separation of the individual from the rest of society can foster growth and maturity in the individual at the same time that they raise questions about individual obligations to the community. The chapters in this book are tied together by their attention to this underlying theme of social distance and separation. Thus, each of the chapters deals with a different set of *specific* issues, but the *general* theme remains the same.

The first two chapters constitute a broad introduction to the theorists. Chapter 1 explains the practical value of theory; presents an overview of core elements from the theories of Marx, Durkheim, Simmel, and Weber; and briefly suggests how their ideas pertain to contemporary issues. Chapter 2 analyzes major features of modern society from the point of view of classical theory and suggests how even postmodern qualities might be accounted for by such theory. This chapter also begins the discussion of the social distance and separation theme by highlighting what each of the theorists viewed as the principal sources of integration and disintegration in society.

The remainder of the chapters concentrate on different specific issues as exemplars of social distance. Each issue is presented and then analyzed using the ideas of the four theorists. Not all the theorists are used in the examination of each issue, but there is always more than one used, thereby making comparisons between theorists possible. Chapter 3 addresses different aspects of the dynamic relationship between individuals and society, focusing on the conflict between the rights of individuals and their obligations to society; the conversion, through the Internet, of the stuff of private lives into public information; and individual separation from society as a source of suicide. Chapter 4 analyzes group separations that occur in space, principally gated communities and racial ghettos. The nature and roots of social and political distance that is created between individuals, others, and institutions are discussed in Chapter 5. Political corruption, cynicism, and distrust reflect the roles played by values, bureaucratic structure, and capitalism in the United States. Chapter 6 views separation and alienation from both personal and social perspectives by examining the trend to see individuals as commodities in the worlds of beauty, entertainment, and medicine. Finally, Chapter 7 discusses the separation that can occur because of discrepancies in economic resources between individuals and groups. Inequalities in income and wealth are especially significant due to their connections with other problems of social distance and separation addressed throughout the book. As a way of concluding the book's main argument, A Summing Up brings together some general observations about the value and limitations of each theorist for understanding modern society.

I have tried to make this book user-friendly. Theory is rarely fun reading for students; consequently, I have included several features that should make the reading not only easier but more interesting. For example, I (1) avoid unnecessary use of jargon, (2) present a Chapter in Brief at the beginning of each chapter to highlight the content of the chapter, (3) present a table at the end of each chapter that summarizes the basic ideas used from each theorist on each chapter issue,

(4) include some chapter-ending Questions to Ponder for discussion inside or outside the classroom, and (5) include a glossary of the basic terms used by the classical theorists. The latter terms are boldfaced the first time they appear in the text.

SUGGESTIONS FOR USING THE BOOK

Living Theory can be effectively used in several ways. First, it may be included as a supplementary text when students have already had a theory course or in the second half of a classical social theory course after the students have become somewhat familiar with Marx, Durkheim, Simmel, and Weber. The book will not only reinforce what students have learned but it will also solidify theoretical ideas by demonstrating how they apply to issues students have heard about in the popular press. By reading the text, students will also be able to compare the arguments of different theorists on the same issue. This will help in assessing the comparative strengths and weaknesses of each theorist. Another potential usage is in courses on social problems or U.S. society that incorporate an interest in understanding how classical thinkers might have approached contemporary issues.

The book can be read straight through as written. A third way to use this book is for acquainting beginning students with the basic arguments and applications of four classical theorists. If used in this way, the Contents, Chapters in Brief, and comparative charts at the ends of Chapters 3 through 7 will help identify those sections that focus on given theorists. By reading the sections on Marx, Durkheim, Simmel, and Weber separately, students can avoid confusing the theorists yet still see how the ideas of these scholars can be applied to everyday issues.

Producing any manuscript is always a collective effort. Standing in the background are a number of individuals who kindly let me use their time and expertise to complete the book. In order to help ensure that the writing would be accessible to undergraduates, I asked two very different, but very good, students to read the entire manuscript. I thank Megan Dishong and Bruce Clayton for their frequent critical, supportive, and insightful comments. I also appreciate the research work of Gretchen Maier. My colleagues David McConnell and Heather Fitz Gibbon are always helpful and available; each of them commented extensively on several chapters. I want them to know that I am grateful for their help. In addition to several outside reviewers who remarked on the initial prospectus for the text, I wish to thank Mary L. Donaghy (Arkansas State University) and Jan Smith (Ohio Wesleyan University) for their efforts as reviewers in helping me to write a better book. I hope that the finished product reflects most of their very constructive comments and criticisms. Sarah Kelbaugh at Allyn and Bacon and my copyeditor Lynda Griffiths at TKM Productions have proven again, as in the past, to be wonderful sources of support and suggestions. Being the sole author, I cannot blame any of the book's faults on others. They can only be held responsible for its strengths. Finally, I wish to thank The College of Wooster for its generous sabbatical program. Without this program, I would still be writing the first chapter.

THE CONTEMPORARY
RELEVANCE OF OLD THEORIES

CHAPTER IN BRIEF

- **INTRODUCTION**
examples and sources of divisiveness
in society; role of media; diversity
and freedom as sources of disunity and
strength; issues of separation and unity

- **ORGANIZATION OF THE BOOK**

- **SYMPTOMS OF STRAIN AND CHANGE**

- **THE VALUE OF THEORY AND
  THEORIES OF VALUE**
meaning of social theory; theories as
explanations and models; practical importance of theory; reasons for choice of
theorists

- **THE RELEVANCE OF
  THEORIES PAST: A PRIMER ON
  THEIR PERSPECTIVES**
The View from Marx's Eyes: Marx's
concerns; role of economy in structure
and change; dialectical pattern of change;
exploitative economic relations; alienation and ideology. *The View from
Durkeim's Eyes:* study of social facts;
division of labor as moral phenomenon;
positive roles of education and state; need
for morality and rules; dangers of excessive individualism. *The View from Simmel's Eyes:* conflict as necessary; society
as outcome of opposing forces; nature of
social forms; money and metropolis as
forms; city as rational and objective;
social distance; effects of size on group.
The View from Weber's Eyes: rationalization and disenchantment of modern life;
decline of ultimate values; society as iron
cage; bureaucracy and capitalism; class
and status; work ethic

INTRODUCTION

This is a book about dimensions and causes of social unity and separation in the
contemporary United States. More specifically, the focus is on how issues revolv-
ing around (1) an attachment to community, (2) the separation of groups, (3) feelings of connection to government, (4) the body as an object, and (5) inequality

1

among individuals in the United States today might be better understood through application of the ideas of several classical social theorists. The general themes of social unity and disunity reverberate in the work of these scholars. Karl Marx, Emile Durkheim, Georg Simmel, and Max Weber all wrote in the mid to late nineteenth century, and, with the exception of Marx, into the early twentieth century while modern industrial society was still developing. Yet, their ideas can enhance our understanding of modern, and even postmodern, industrial society as we enter the twenty-first century. Perhaps the writings of these scholars can even illuminate our paths to solutions for many of the social problems that plague our society.

This is not to say that classical theory is without faults. Indeed, on several occasions, I note its inadequacies and omissions as it applies to contemporary society. Nor is it to say that social theory has not changed or developed since the days of the classicists. It certainly has. Many contemporary theorists have built on the work of classical theorists and served as their modern interpreters. Even without its modern updating, however, classical theory still speaks directly to the issues being explored here. This is a book about the power of classical theory to shed light on several troublesome contemporary issues. To add contemporary theories would only make discussion of the issues more complicated and mute the real contribution of classical theory to understanding present society. In many ways, classical theory can stand on its own two feet.

ORGANIZATION OF THE BOOK

This chapter presents a preliminary glimpse of some of the issues of disunity to be addressed more fully in later chapters, followed by a demonstration of the usefulness of social theory in general and the classical theorists in particular. It ends with a brief overview of major emphases in the work of Marx, Durkheim, Simmel, and Weber. Chapter 2 further explores the general perspective of these theorists on contemporary society, and begins a more in-depth discussion of what they viewed as main sources of unity and disunity in society. This discussion will lay the foundation for the analyses of specific areas of disunity and unity that follow in Chapters 3 through 7.

SYMPTOMS OF STRAIN AND CHANGE

There are times when it appears undeniable that our society is falling apart. The signs pop up in different areas. The number of child murderers appears to be on the rise, and a national expert has predicted an epidemic of violence by children.

Between 1985 and 1994, the number of juveniles arrested for murder increased about 150 percent.[1] At the present rate, there are expected to be at least 5,000 teen murderers in the year 2005. As a possible source, some experts point to children being raised without consciences and doing what they want regardless of the consequences for others. Others point to a decline in values and morals in society as a whole. President Clinton's recent problems involving sexual escapades with a White House intern have further highlighted the controversy about whether morality is presently under siege.

The fact that books such as *The Moral Compass* and *The Book of Virtues* can make the nonfiction best-sellers' list is an indication that the morals argument has struck a chord among Americans. Indeed, in 1995, 70 percent of a nationwide sample of adults felt that the country was experiencing a decline in moral and ethical standards.[2] Recent articles and symposia have also decried the "dissolution of shared moral and religious values" and "the disappearance of community or civil society in contemporary American life."[3] At least one scholar has concluded from evidence that the United States is experiencing a "wilding epidemic."[4] "Wilding" refers to selfish, individualistic behavior that is harmful to others. It is committed without a sense of guilt by the powerful and the powerless, the rich and the poor, black and white, and it can range from senseless beatings of innocent citizens to the abuse of office for personal gain. Derber traces the source of wilding in the United States to extreme individualism: It "is individualism run amok, and the wilding epidemic is the face of America's individualistic culture in an advanced state of disrepair."[5]

At the same time that concerns about declines in values have arisen, debates flourish about the need to place restraints on legal and illegal immigration because of concerns about too many people with too many differences, about job competition, about drains on welfare funds as well as educational and health resources, and because of downright racism. The presence of so many different cultural groups in the United States has also spurred debates about English as a national language and Ebonics as a legitimate language, about the necessity and fairness of affirmative action, and about the teaching of multiculturalism in schools. These conflicts are representative of cultural differences that appear to distance groups from each other.

Divisions in social life also abound. Segregation remains largely intact and economic inequality has increased. The growing popularity of walled or gated communities is only one indication of the desire of generally better-off individuals to choose a peaceful, more idyllic life seemingly removed from the social problems of city life. On the political front, continued revelations about illegal political contributions, influence peddling, and misuse of political offices does little to hearten the average person. Such discoveries encourage cynicism and distrust, and thereby weaken attachment to our role as citizens and create greater distance between ourselves and government. A government *of and for the people* becomes a government *different from and against the people*. Recent polls suggest that less than 1 in 7 citizens have a lot of confidence in the White House, and about 7 of 10 feel that most public officeholders do not really care about the problems of the person on the street. Almost half of those polled rate members of Congress as being low or very low in honesty and ethics.[6] These widespread feelings are fed by the media, which are eager to maintain or increase the size of their audiences. "Dirty laundry," as a song suggests, includes the search by the media for sensationalistic stories highlighting the dark side of U.S. life.

Watching the news on TV or reading a newsmagazine or newspaper, we are exposed to a parade of stories that emphasize the negative and divisive forces in our society. Often, the events are depicted because they are rare rather than common occurrences. At other times, however, news items discuss problems that are deep or widespread. The proliferation of negative news items in the media has prompted some to suggest that, for our own mental health, we take a holiday from reading or watching the news once a week.

There are at least two basic ways to look at these stories. It is generally the negative side that is emphasized because they often address serious issues that need to be confronted. But on the positive side, they also reflect what many consider to be positive trademarks of our society—its social and cultural diversity, tolerance, openness, and freedom of choice. These features are double-edged swords. Diversity, for example, rather than just being viewed as a source of division and disunity, is also a source of social strength, cultural richness, and adaptability for a society. That very freedom and openness makes it possible for individuals to go their separate ways but also to live in their own private cocoons without active regard for the lives of others. Openness and freedom also permit separate and often antagonistic groups to develop and flourish within a single society. This means that groups that represent racist interests and those that fight racism, as well as those with liberal, radical, conservative, or reactionary perspectives, exist alongside each other. Some want nothing to do with the others. Recent stories have related the widespread existence of underground militias and separatist groups that do not recognize the full authority and legitimacy of the federal government or that wish to set up their own countries. Tolerance encourages the social and cultural differences that are a source of creativity and dynamism but also a major cause of social conflicts and divisiveness.

Clearly, there are costs and benefits to living in a capitalist and democratic society. We are both victims and benefactors of society, and we are its creators as well as its creations. Society is not falling apart, but neither is it static. Because of its dynamism and great sociocultural diversity, there is always a question about how a society with so many subcultural groups, economic classes, religious camps, and political constituencies can avoid falling apart and maintain a level of cohesion that permits it to function effectively without snuffing out individual creativity and differences. How can the center hold in the face of so many differences? Do we even need to have a center to have cohesion? Can there be more than one center? Can individuals be separate and free and still be an effective part of a unified society? Classical theorists have provided some answers to these questions. Core concepts used by the theorists are highlighted throughout the text and summarized in the Glossary at the end of the book.

THE VALUE OF THEORY AND
THEORIES OF VALUE

How is theory helpful, and why are Marx, Durkheim, Simmel, and Weber especially helpful in understanding our present social life and its problems? There is always a question about how "theory" can really help us understand and grapple with "real-life" problems. In this view, theory is something impractical, residing in the realm of philosophy, with little connection to the facts of the concrete world.[7] Theorists are often viewed as "armchair" people who theorize about the world to little effect. These are common views of people outside academia. As an example, in the preface of her recent book, *Americans No More,* in which she takes up the issue of social and cultural disunity and its implication for citizenship, Georgie Anne Geyer takes pains to distance herself from being considered a mere theorist by emphasizing her real-life experiences as a journalist as the basis for her claims: "But this book does not pretend to reflect the world of the theoretician or philosopher. These words are the honed and considered thoughts of a highly trained and experienced observer.... Moreover, as a journalist, I am interested in exploring what we *can* know, not in theorizing or speculating about what we don't or cannot know."[8] This statement offers a faulty stereotype of theory and theorists. Modern social theorists are not ungrounded philosophers nor are theory and speculation the same thing. Nothing could be further from the truth. I share many of the same concerns as Geyer, but her comments on theory betray a common misunderstanding of its nature and possibilities. Theories are *explanations* or sometimes *models* for understanding reality.

As *explanations,* social theories suggest causes for behaviors, events, and social structures. All of us carry around theories in our heads about why certain things are as they are—*why* people commit murders, *why* people get laid off from work, *why* people marry each other, *why* racial groups do not get along with each other, and so on. The trouble is that these informal, unorganized theories are usually not well thought out, nor are they based on an abundance of evidence systematically collected. In contrast, the selection of causes in scientific theories is generally based on evidence drawn from thorough examinations of history, observations, and empirical scientific studies rather than drawn out of the thin air while ruminating in some easy-chair.

Identification of causes is at the heart of theories, and, of course, knowledge about causes is of great practical importance if we are interested in creating, enhancing, reinforcing, reducing, or eliminating a given situation or behavior. Consider poverty, or creativity, or group solidarity, or urban decay, or any other phenomenon. If we want to do something about any of these for the long run, we need to understand their causes. To change something, it is generally desirable to be able to identify its roots rather than to deal just with its symptoms or effects. Too often, U.S. policymakers focus on dealing with social problems *after* they have appeared or been in existence for a long time, and then deal only with the symptoms rather than addressing and doing something about the causes. To address those causes—to understand *why* there is more teenage murder, *why* so many people are politically apathetic or cynical, *why* the individual and community so often appear to be at odds with each other—requires explanations (theories) of these phenomena and an understanding of their effects for society and individuals. This makes theories very practical, indeed. What makes them even more helpful is that scientific theories are never fully closed because they are always open to change arising from new evidence.

In addition to being explanations, theories can also be models. As *models,* theories are like metaphors in that they attempt to identify and depict core patterns present in social life. If we argue that society "is like a body where every part contributes to the whole" or that society "is like a battlefield on which individuals and groups compete for scarce resources" or that society "is like a complex computer in which individuals are tied together by lines of communication," we are using theories as models because we are choosing to see society in a particular way. Consequently, like a template or overlay, effective theories mirror actual social arrangements. But they are not a substitute for them because models are *approximations* about how societies work or are organized. Some approximations, of course, are more effective than others.

How can using theories as models be practical? Consider a manager in a corporation trying to understand a problem of turnover, low productivity, or conflict within his or her department. *How he or she views the organization or department* will directly affect the approach taken to deal with the problem. For example, seeing the organization as a machine would encourage the manager to examine the rules and division of labor that affect how a well-oiled machine will run, whereas seeing the corporation as a platform for class struggle will suggest focusing on potential elements of exploitation between dominant and subordinate groups as a possible source for problems. Familiarity with a variety of models and willingness to switch among them make it more likely that a solution will be found by the manager. Theories as models have pragmatic consequences.

As explanations, theories are roadmaps that allow us to travel through social reality and understand its terrain. At the same time, the roads provided by a theory limit where we go. Some roadmaps are better than others. What questions we ask, what we see, and how we interpret and explain it is limited by the theoretical framework we are using.

Considering its uses as an explanation and a model, nothing is more practical than a good theory. Theories are not just for academics or scholars who want to publish in obscure journals to impress their colleagues. They are of use to the average person who wishes to understand why events happen, or trends occur, or people behave as they do. Perhaps C. Wright Mills put it best in *The Sociological Imagination* when he said that a social science should aim at helping people understand their "private troubles" in terms of "public issues." These public issues refer to characteristics of social structures in the society, or a society's history, or its place in development. Knowledge of each of these helps us understand why we are the way we are personally and why, at particular times in our lives, things happen to us that we do not understand. In essence, Mills believed that an adequate social science should have practical importance for the average citizen.

The "sociological imagination," as Mills called it, allows us to understand our personal predicaments by reference to wider events and institutions. It forces us to look around us for broader social conditions and processes. Classical social theorists were concerned with those public issues, with analyzing and understanding the structure of modern society in the context of its historical development. This is a central premise of the present book: showing how broad theories of society can help us understand what is going on in contemporary U.S. society.

Why should the theories of Marx, Durkheim, Simmel, and Weber be selected for use? What is so practical about them? One reason for their selection lies in the fact that all these theorists were living in societies undergoing wide-ranging social changes, as we are presently doing in the United States. Thus, the ideas that sprang from each may have continued relevance for us. I will say more about this later. A second reason is that, in his own way, each theorist was concerned with the character and direction of modern society, and tried to identify and explain core elements of it. Since they all identified many integral and continuing aspects of society (e.g., division of labor, bureaucracy, city life), their ideas should still be viable. Moreover, since each theorist differed in specific aspects of his approach, the use of all of them provides us with a multifaceted lens through which to view contemporary society. A third reason for selecting these theorists is that all of them in varying degrees were involved in the societies of their time. They were not simply armchair theorists. Marx was involved in newspaper work and workers' organizations in Germany and elsewhere. Weber was actively involved in a variety of German political activities and even worked on a draft of a constitution for the country. French theorist Durkheim, although largely an academic, encouraged scientists to become socially involved when basic principles were at stake. He personally came to the defense of Alfred Dreyfus, a young Jewish officer who had been falsely accused of giving military information to the Germans. Simmel, a friend of Weber's, reached out to nonacademic audiences with his interests in topics of relevance in everyone's lives—love, secrecy, conflict, and life in the city. Thus, all of these theorists were in touch with real concerns in their societies.

One of the objections to using only these theorists is that they were all European White males (plus, they are all long dead). The fact that they were all European White males suggests that their perspectives were either all uniform or biased in some way. The point should be made that each theorist was personally different. Simmel, for example, paid practical consequences for being Jewish, a group despised by anti-Semites in nineteenth-century Germany. Partly because of the common popularity and seemingly disorganized nature of his work, he was not a mainstream, honored academic, as were Weber and Durkheim during their lifetimes. Marx, of course, was hardly mainstream, being suppressed in Germany and kicked out of France for his radical views, and finding himself forced to scrape for a living and accept funds from his friend, Frederick Engels, to keep his family and himself going. The point is that the differing conditions of the life of each of these theorists helped create their different perspectives about how the world worked. They were not the same, nor are their perspectives. But each lived in a society wrestling with cataclysmic changes and social conflict. As such, they provided us with ideas about the nature of social changes, their causes, directions, and consequences. All were concerned about the ultimate fate of modern culture.

A brief look at what was going on in their societies at the time will help us understand the theorists' concerns.[9] The social conditions in France and Germany in the last half of the nineteenth and early part of the twentieth centuries were different. Briefly, consider France in the latter half of the nineteenth century. Since its great Revolution of 1789, France had moved through a variety of significant political, social, and economic circumstances. In the years shortly before Durkheim's birth in 1858, France's political fortunes were in the hands of Louis Napoleon's Second Empire, which aimed to rescue the country from its recent political and economic crises by standing for stability and security. Lasting until 1870, the Empire was replaced by the Third Republic in 1871 after a disastrous war with Germany and a workers' revolt in Paris. The widespread desire in the country was for a restoration of internal order, a more pleasant life where an average person could work in peace at a steady job. The Third Republic contained both liberal and extremely conservative elements. The latter, like many today in the United States concerned with our own problems, considered the problems associated with the war and revolt of 1870 to be largely the product of a lack of morals and discipline, and thus desired a restoration of such virtues. On the other hand, a variety of conflicting leftist groups felt greater freedom and opportunity were needed, and sought a separation of church and state as well as greater influence for unions and workers.

Economically, France was becoming an industrial power, although more slowly than either England or Germany. Iron and steel mills, chemical industries, and mechanization proceeded, but most factories, like most farms in France, were small. In this sense, the industrial and agricultural economies were more scattered than in other more powerful industrial countries. In a word, just before and during Durkheim's life, France had experienced a series of political and religious battles among various political camps and was undergoing the process of industrialization with all its attendant problems. Issues of power and freedom, unrest and stability, morality and deception, city and farm, and industrial development were wondered and debated about then as they are in U.S. society today.

Germany had its own specific problems with which to contend, but in a general sense it too had to deal with religious conflicts, political and cultural divisions, questions of power and freedom, industrial development, and divisions between classes. During Marx's early adult life, Germany was in political disarray, with revolutions occurring in most German states in the year of *The Communist Manifesto* (1848). Nationalism was also an issue in late nineteenth-century Germany. Internal divisions festered among Protestants, Catholics, and Jews, and between liberals and conservatives, ruling nationalities and minorities (Poles, Danes, French, foreign workers), industrial magnates and workers, and those who advocated the rule of law and those who sought the rule of might.

One of the most difficult tasks facing Germany at this time was the problem of the integration of various groups into a unified Germany. Weber, a prominent scholar by this time, was witness to these conflicts, as was his friend Simmel, who experienced anti-Semitism firsthand. Concurrent with the divisions haunting Germany were growths in industrialization, population, and cities. The problems related to the exploitative relationship between the classes in the new industrial order, a topic of concern to both Weber and Marx, were due in part to the fact that the industrial growth was taking place within the context of a feudal, Prussian, authoritarian institutional regime. Industry and technology were modernizing, but the systems of control remained traditional. In sweeping terms, the controlling forces in the Germany of Weber and Simmel were heavily conservative, authoritarian, nationalistic, imperialist, and expansionist. Those in control ruled with an iron hand.

The issues of political turmoil, social divisiveness, and socioeconomic change just discussed are all issues of continuing relevance in the United States. The seesaws of order and change, control and freedom, tradition and modernity, and unity and division exist in all modern societies, including the United States. As in France, the direction of change is a subject of dispute between different political and economic factions. Conservatives desire more order, discipline, and morality, whereas radicals seek greater personal liberty and power for individuals. Some want a greater separation of church and state in the United States, yet others desire a more religion-centered government. Workers want more rights and benefits, while governmental leaders often view the workers as agitators damaging our national project. As in nineteenth-century Europe, there is also an ideological division between those living in the cities and those living in the country, between the forces of urban/industrial development and rural/agricultural maintenance. More specifically, racial and religious prejudice as well as conflicts among political factions, among owners, managers, and workers, between nationalist/patriotic and ethnic sympathies, among regions, and between foreigners and native citizens continue in this country. Consequently, the issues of concern to those classical theorists who lived through them are those with which we still wrestle. This alone makes their perspectives highly relevant to understanding the problems of the United States as we enter the twenty-first century. What, specifically, does each of these theorists have to offer?

THE RELEVANCE OF THEORIES PAST: A PRIMER ON THEIR PERSPECTIVES

Next is a selective summary of essential elements in the perspectives of Marx, Simmel, Weber, and Durkheim. I do not intend this to be a thorough discussion of all their ideas, but rather a highlighting of those substantive aspects that are of particular relevance for understanding the character and trends of modern society. A discussion of the elements that unite and divide the United States forms the overall theme of this book, and each theorist has provided a viewpoint for understanding these issues.

The View from Marx's Eyes

Karl Marx (1818–1883) came of age at a time when much of Europe was in a period of tumultuous change. He was born in a small town in Prussia about 30 years after the French Revolution. Industrialization was proceeding quickly in much of Europe. In the early nineteenth century, Germany was still a group of competing states containing a variety of divisions between conflicting social and cultural groups. Prussia was the most authoritarian of these states. At midcentury and later, Germany was to experience many of the revolts and conflicts arising in newly industrializing countries. As a result, everywhere Marx looked there were problems in society. Thus, mirroring their existence in the society around him and reflecting his own experiences as an exile, Marx focused on sources of change, power, and conflict in industrial and capitalist society, their manifestations, and future trends associated with them. The causes of stability and change in modern society and the direction of change were overarching themes in Marx's work.

These questions were of central importance to Marx, and they are of concern today to people who think about U.S. society and wonder or worry about its future. A healthy stability, some feel, requires a solid institutional basis—cohesive families, a growing economy, and competent government. High divorce and illegitimacy rates, unsettling shifts in economic sectors, and cynicism about government priorities and competence are signs to many of the absence of positive stability and societal direction. Some see the United States as being adrift because of a lack of strong moral values, whereas others view technological changes as being too rapid, so much so that the average person has a hard time keeping up with them. The result is that the skills people have learned become rapidly outdated and retooling is necessary. For example, no sooner does one purchase a personal computer than it becomes out of date. Corporate leaders in technology (e.g., Microsoft) prosper, while many middle-level managers and lower-level workers are left scrambling for their jobs or looking for new ones. Regardless, however, of whether one interprets these conditions and changes positively or negatively in the long term, there is little doubt about the existence of these changes and the recurrent questions about the stability and direction of U.S. society, and the meaning of these changes for average people. These questions seem especially relevant as we enter the twenty-first century.

Marx believed that sources of stability and change in **capitalist society** are to be found in the nature of **class** relationships and processes inherent in the capitalist economy. The economic structure forms the basis or **substructure** of society. Marx was a materialist in that he believed that what people concretely do in the economy and how they relate to each other and nature shapes their lives and their consciousness. Although noneconomic institutions can have immediate and particular impacts on what happens in a society, economic factors ultimately play a disproportionate role in shaping the structure of a society and the behavior of those within it. Broadly, changes in technology and economic development and resulting contradictions in relationships *within* the structure of a society bring about problems in relationships between groups, and these problems eventually lead to changes in the structure of a society. This **dialectic** of change means that a proper understanding of society's structure requires a historical perspective. For example, rapid advancements within a particular technology or industry may allow for greater production or higher standards of living. These advancements may require changes in the relationships among workers, or between workers and management in companies, or between employees and owners of the technology, so that the entire society may benefit from these advancements. But these changes do not occur easily, resulting in built-in and often violent conflicts between different groups. Thus, the major causes of change in societies are internal in nature.

Modern industrial technology itself was not viewed by Marx as inherently evil. Rather, it was the outdated, exploitative economic and social relationships in capitalist society that continued to cause problems. When workers strike today for greater control over their jobs or complain about excessive executive incomes while workers' wages stagnate, they are manifesting conditions and feelings that were of central concern to Marx. Individuals cannot reach their full potential as human beings because they are restricted by the relationships in which they are enmeshed. **Alienation** from others and from oneself, and even faulty values, are the result. True human community cannot develop until these relationships are changed. Unfortunately, the dominant beliefs and the state **ideology** present in a society at any given time directly reflect the dominant/subordinate relationships between owners and workers found in the economy. Thus, they justify and explain away these existing relationships. The more effective the dominant ideology of the powerful is, the more difficult change becomes. But as material conditions within the economy change, the viability of existing ideologies and old rationalizations are undermined.

Marx believed that people behave the way they do because of the nature of their involvement in economic relationships. This means that for relationships to become more humane, capitalism must change. In the meantime, when conditions clearly drive groups of people apart, the people will often organize to protect or advance their own economic interests. Today, even many physicians are unionizing because they see the managed-care movement in U.S. medicine as being harmful to their own economic interests. In sum, for Marx, the keys to individual behavior, social stability, community, and change and its direction are to be found in the economic relationships that structure U.S. society.

The View from Durkheim's Eyes

In many ways, like Marx, Emile Durkheim (1858–1917) saw the wellsprings of behavior, stability, community, and change as being in social-structural and institutional conditions. Also like Marx, Durkheim was concerned with the effects of external social constraints, what he called **social facts,** on behavior. Beyond these highly broad similarities, however, Durkheim viewed the principal and specific sources of social cohesion, community, change, and problems much differently than Marx. The concerns abroad in nineteenth-century France—for social order, problems of industrial development, the proper role of government, and religious/moral influence in public life—were of great importance to Durkheim, and informed the emphases in his studies.

As noted, Durkheim focused on the nature and effects of social facts on group arrangements and individual behavior. The development and impact of the **division of labor** in industrial society, and the role of religion and morality in social life were among his most significant subjects. An intricate, specialized division of labor is a defining property of modern society, and it has both individualizing and integrating effects. Although it aids in allowing individual differences and talents to develop more fully, thereby enhancing human freedom, it also creates interdependency between specialists. Individual personality and an ethos of individualism develop along with the division of labor, which in turn enhances personal freedom. This interdependency increases our awareness of how much we rely on others and leads to the development of rules governing our relationships with others. Consequently, the division of labor is a source of morality in modern society. "In short, since the division of labor becomes the chief source of social solidarity, it becomes, at the same time, the foundation of the moral order."[10] Anything that ties us to others and forces us to take them into account is considered a moral phenomenon by Durkheim. The twin effects of individuality and interdependency demonstrated in the division of labor are often viewed in conflict today, with many conservatives arguing that the emphasis on individual rights has gone too far because it has been at the expense of obligations to others and the community as a whole.

According to Durkheim, the division of labor, as it eventually will develop, will reflect real ability differences between individuals. Thus, there will be a match between social position and individual talent. Until that time, the division of labor can suffer from abnormalities that will disappear as industrial society progresses. Incompetent people can be found in positions of influence, while talented individuals languish in jobs that do not take advantage of their abilities and out of which they find it difficult to move.

As the division of labor progresses and people become more unique and the rules governing their relationships become extensive, the state will grow. The state serves primarily as a protector of individual freedom and thus, in contrast to Marx, is viewed positively by Durkheim. Like the state, the educational institution also performs a vital role in society through its socialization of a **secular morality** in youth. Rather than focusing on duties toward God, this rational morality focuses on the proper relationship between individuals in society. For Durkheim, public schools are the crucibles in which the moral development of children is formed.

In essence, institutions such as religion, the state, and education help relationships between individuals to go on in a predictable and smooth fashion, and serve to create civilized individuals who fit easily into the structure of society. Society must be *in the individual* just as the individual is *in society*. Development of the social nature of individuals becomes more important as society advances. Indeed, when an individual does not fit in well (i.e., is poorly integrated into society), pathology results. When there is a lack of direction in society in general because of the absence of effective guidelines, structural and personal disorganization result. Morality and the presence of rules are necessary as a basis for the civilization of a society and for the happiness of individuals. They serve to temper our natural egoism by promoting knowledge of our responsibilities to others and placing limits on our own desires. Such limitations are necessary for a rational, happy life. The absence of effective guidelines in society creates a condition of **anomie,** or social confusion.

In sum, Durkheim saw the division of labor in modern society becoming increasingly specialized, the result being a more complex society and the creation of people who are more distinctive and individualized. This individualization, if carried out too far, can be dangerous to both individuals and society. Consequently, institutions must work to develop rules and socialization procedures that ensure that individuals will be truly social in their natures. When people today complain about a lack of discipline in homes and schools and a general lack of morality in society, and view these as a principal factor in the "wilding" of society, they are echoing a concern that Durkheim had almost a century ago.

The View from Simmel's Eyes

Durkheim saw conflict diminishing as society progressed, but Georg Simmel (1858–1918) argued that conflict in a variety of forms is built into all societies, and like all aspects of modern life, has both positive and negative elements. It is not something that can be or should be eliminated from society.

Simmel dabbled in a wide variety of topics of concern to most of us in our everyday lives: power, conflict, love, secrecy, strangeness, money, city life, and small and large group memberships. He was deeply interested in outlining the nature and consequences of each of these. Modern conflict theory derives many of its ideas from Simmel. Instead of seeing it as a problem to be eliminated, Simmel saw conflict as necessary for society in part because, as a reaction to divisive forces, it is a means to bring about unity. Moreover, it gives form to society: "So society, too, in order to attain a determinate shape, needs some quantitative ratio of harmony and disharmony, of association and competition, of favorable and unfavorable tendencies."[11] Individuals, as well, gain their identities because of conflicts with others and society. It is in the face of challenges and disputes that we develop and find out who we are. A vital, dynamic, modern society is bound to have a variety of conflicts going on. In the long run, conflicts are a means for solving problems. They clear the air.

The internal **dialectic** or blending of opposing forces is a recurrent theme in Simmel's theories. Positives and negatives are always mixed, as in the following examples:

- Conflict unites groups as it separates them from others, and destroys as it creates relationships.
- Domination oppresses and keeps people apart at the same time that individuals seek to be dominated.
- Individuals create culture but culture as a separate thing can then turn and dominate them. As in *Frankenstein,* the creator becomes the dominated. Simmel describes this as a *domination of objective over subjective culture.*
- Because it is a universal mode of exchange, money frees individuals to purchase a wide variety of goods, but, because everything has its price, it also degrades the qualitative value those goods have for individuals. As we can more easily possess them, our attachment to them becomes more shallow.
- Life in the city allows individuals to be themselves but it also forces them to limit their emotions.
- Strangers are people who, by definition, are distant from us but also close in that we will often reveal to a stranger things we would not tell someone near to us.
- Love unites two individuals but is also the source of the most intense hatreds and divisions.

Life's interactions are full of opposites such as those just cited. These conflicts and contradictions provide a dynamism to social life and give it *form*. Most basically, **forms** are structures or modes of interaction that are analytically distinct from their content.

Two of the principal forms found in modern society are money and the metropolis. As forms, money and cities tie people together in specific ways, thereby structuring their connections with each other. Simmel viewed the city as "the point of concentration of modernity" and saw the money economy as the instrument of "the diffusion of modernity throughout society."[12] The city is home to the modern economy, with its emphasis on elaborate rational-economic relationships and its intricate division of labor. But it is primarily the effects of city life on individuals and their inner lives that drew Simmel's attention. He felt that the increased emphasis in modern society on (1) *intellect,* (2) *calculation,* (3) *quantifying* of relationships, (4) *science,* (5) *"matter-of-fact"* money relationships, (6) *punctuality,* and (7) submission to *external rules* was concentrated in the city. These help account for the dominance of an **objective spirit** in urban centers. All this has intimate psychological and social effects on the city's residents. In large, complex, bustling cities, individuals are unavoidably bombarded with all kinds of stimulation from every direction. Almost as a defense mechanism, individuals take on a **blasé,** or matter-of-fact, unconcerned attitude as a response to the overstimulation. At the same time, the abundance of variety and openness in the city allows individuality to prosper. Uniqueness grows and people adopt fashions to make subjective statements about who they are.

Applying these ideas to the United States today, people largely remain strangers to each other despite being physically close. Cool intellect dictates more of one's reactions; hotter emotional responses are muted. A growing distance occurs between the "mind" (rational) and "soul" (nonrational) as the intellectualization of experience predominates over the direct subjective experience of objects. We learn about things by reading about them, being lectured about them, watching TV, or going online instead of having direct contact and experiences with objects. The "spin" on events and experiences comes from the media. In essence, much comes between us and that which we wish to experience.

As the last statement suggests, social distance was a topic of great interest to Simmel, as were the arrangements of groups and individuals in spatial areas. Every spatial area has a distinctive identity, or uniqueness. Spatial areas are set off by boundaries, and areas may arise as expressions of political, social, or economic relationships. The concentrations of individuals from specific ethnic or status groups in particular areas of modern cities provide illustrations of Simmel's point.

Simmel's fascination with cities shows his interest in the separate effects of size on social relationships. Relationships in small groups generally demand total involvement of one's personality. Consequently, in Simmel's view, feelings are stronger and radicalism is more likely in smaller groups. It is different in large groups. To remain unified, larger groups require more elaborate ways to integrate (e.g., a complex division of labor). What works in a small group does not work in a large one. "Personal relations," which tie people together in small groups, are the opposite of "the distance and coolness of objective and abstract norms without which the large group cannot exist."[13]

Simmel is intriguingly different from the other theorists being considered here because of his fascination with the unique, detailed aspects of social relationships so often found in everyday contemporary life. His focus on the paradoxes of social life along with the features and psychological meaning of modern life for individuals make him especially relevant for understanding what is going on in present-day urban centers.

The View from Weber's Eyes

Max Weber (1881–1961) and Georg Simmel were friends who shared ideas and acquaintances. While Simmel tried to uncover universal forms that could be applied in any historical situation, Weber focused on the historically specific aspects of societies. He did not believe in the existence of universal laws that would apply to any society. Despite these different assumptions, both men were concerned with the fate and meaning of modern culture as well as defining the essential features of modern society. This included what both perceived to be the increasing **rationalization** of life. As science sheds more and more light on daily life, Weber argued, a disenchantment occurs. Much of the mystery and wonder of life disappears. The simultaneous decline of the **nonrational** and actions motivated by ultimate values and the rise in purely calculative behavior is a view of modern society shared by both Simmel and Weber.[14] **Purposively rational action** based on calculation and the conscious intellectual weighing of means and ends in making decisions has become more predominant and has supplanted action based on basic values and emotions: "The fate of our times is characterized by rationalization and intellectualization and, above all, by the 'disenchantment of the world.' Precisely the ultimate and most sublime values have retreated from public life either into the transcendental realm of mystic life or into the brotherliness of direct and personal human relations."[15] Because they give meaning to life, the diminishing of ultimate values in modern public life renders much of it meaningless. A perfected science is not the solution, since science cannot really tell us how to live.

In contrast to Simmel's view of modern culture, which characteristically contained both positive and negative elements, Weber's perspective is more fully negative. We live within an **iron cage,** a hardened shell of rationalization and calculation from which there is no escape. We live in a society dominated by the rational and hierarchical authority of large bureaucracies and large states, industrial technology, profit-oriented capitalism and money exchange, and alienating class structure. All of these are symptoms of an impersonal society, one in which personal and emotional elements have been largely removed from public life. The methodical calculation characteristic of modern institutions finds its way into the minds of individuals. As in any good capitalist enterprise, individuals are more occupied with assessing the costs and benefits to themselves in their calculations of how to behave than they are with following a given course out of allegiance to some deeply held value. This fits in well with the other components of our rationalized society.

Many of us spend a substantial proportion of our lives working in large bureaucracies that demand predictable and efficient behavior in the service of their goals. In contrast to the everyday conception of **bureaucracy** as synonymous with red tape, inefficiency, slowness, and bloatedness, Weber coined the concept to refer to a modern organizational form with machinelike efficiency. Its characteristics of written rules and procedures, clear and detailed division of labor, hierarchy of area-specific authority, professional expertise, and career system constitute a social structure aimed at reaching an organization's defined goals in the most cost-effective manner, regardless of what those goals might be. For Weber, this bureaucratic form is *technically* superior to every other form of organization: "The decisive reason for the advance of bureaucratic organization has always been its purely technical superiority over any other form of organization."[16] Its highly "technical" quality symbolizes the rational character of this form of organization. "The more the bureaucracy is 'dehumanized,' the more completely it succeeds in eliminating from official business love, hatred, and all purely personal, irrational, and emotional elements which escape calculation."[17] In bureaucracies, one's authority is based on a formal, or **legal-rational,** position rather than on **tradition,** or personal **charisma.** Traditional organizations run like big families with warm, fuzzy relationships cannot compete against bureaucratic organizations.

Capitalism and bureaucracy are mutually supportive because both demand an overriding spirit of efficiency and rationality to be productive. Capitalism is more profitable when its principal structures are organized bureaucratically, and bureaucracy is supported by the rational, no-nonsense approach of capitalism. Like the marketplace, bureaucracy proceeds without regard for persons. Both are impersonal.

Like capitalism and bureaucracy, **class** has no regard for the personal element. Weber was careful to make a distinction between a group or person's market position, or economic class, and **social status.** The latter refers to one's prestige or social honor as attributed by a community; it is personal. In contrast to classes, status groups normally compose communities with specific lifestyles.

In Weber's view, despite the existence of both status groups and classes in capitalist society, the dominance of the marketplace and money in public life, and the rapid changes taking place in technology and business, mean that economic class differences are more important in today's society than old social status differences based on family name, birthplace, or ethnic background. It is *what you have,* not *who you are* that is important, and employers have much more than workers. Weber agreed with Marx that workers are much more likely to be exploited under capitalism than are employers.

The rational spirit found in capitalism has been underwritten by that seemingly least of businesslike institutions—religion. A particular form of Protestantism, according to Weber, helped give birth to the nose-to-the-grindstone attitude required to be successful in business. This **Protestant-ethic** attitude discouraged members from wasting their time in fun or rest. Hard work and worldly success served as potential signs that God smiled with favor on the person, and thereby lessened the anxiety of not knowing if one was saved or damned. Eventually, as the capitalist spirit took hold and became self-sustaining, the religious roots of the work ethic withered away.

In sum, Weber's keen insights addressed the characteristics of large social structures in society as well as their impact on culture and the inner life of individuals. In modern society, rationalization has become a dominant spirit epitomized in the structures of bureaucracy, capitalism, class, and the work-ethic spirit. A rational, means-ends outlook permeates modern culture and overrides the sensate, emotional, value elements within individuals. In this environment, people become less morally motivated, less caring, and more pragmatic. They are driven less by adherence to basic values regardless of cost than they are by rational assessments of the best ways to be personally and materially successful.

CONCLUSION

Having reviewed the general perspectives of Marx, Durkheim, Simmel, and Weber, it is clear that all of them independently were concerned with developments in modern industrial societies. All examined **centripetal forces** that help to weave the parts of societies together and all identified **centrifugal elements** that drive us apart. The ebb and flow of integrative and disintegrative tendencies is evident in the work of each of these theorists. These tendencies underlie the strengths and dangers built into modern society.

Each of the classical theorists viewed industrial societies as becoming increasingly rational (i.e., as relying more on science, technology, urban centers and industrialism, and less on tradition and religion). Although such a ration holds promise and produces material benefits, especially for some, it also contains dangers, especially for culture and human beings. Those dangers are primarily associated with the decline in the significance of deeply held values, in the emotional, in the soul, and in feelings for others in what it means to be human. In carefully detailing the features of modern society and culture, and in drawing out their consequences, classical theorists, similar yet different, have provided us with tools to understand better many of our current problems and perhaps ways to alleviate them.

In the next chapter, I present a more detailed overview of the central components of modern society as viewed by the classical theorists, and the forces of integration and disintegration within it. Chapter 3 focuses on the paradoxical relationship between the individual and society found in all the theorists. Chapters 4 and 5 continue the theme of disunity and unity, relating classical arguments to the issues of spatial separation between groups and the lack of civility and trust between individuals. The following two chapters address other manifestations of social distance in modern society. In Chapter 6, I examine the use of humans as commodities, and in Chapter 7, I discuss the growing gaps in income and wealth in the United States. Finally, in summing up, I synthesize the general messages for understanding the contemporary United States, gleaned from the classical theorists.

QUESTIONS TO PONDER

1. Based on your own experiences and background, what kinds of informal theories have you developed to explain why individuals and society are as they are?

2. Many of the social problems cited in this chapter drive people apart. What processes or arrangements are at work in society that bring people together?

3. What examples from your own life demonstrate that cold calculation is an important part of social life today? What place do emotions and feelings occupy in present-day society?

CHAPTER 2

THE JANUS-FACED NATURE
OF SOCIETY

CHAPTER IN BRIEF

■ **INTRODUCTION**
historical and holistic perspective of classical theory; features of modern Western society as sources of integration and disintegration

■ **MODERN WESTERN SOCIETY**
core features of society; *Society as Industrial, Urban, and Centralized:* division of labor as alienating (Marx); division of labor as source of interdependence and alienation (Simmel); division of labor as source of unity (Durkheim); economy as centralized (Marx); society as urban (Simmel); *Society as Rational:* bureaucratic state as power center, protector, and representative of capitalists (Weber, Durkheim, Marx); secularization; objective culture in the city (Simmel); views of place of religion (Durkheim, Marx, Weber); *Society as Individualistic:* rise of individualism; differing interpretations (Durkheim, Weber, Simmel)

■ **THE POSTMODERN ELEMENT**
features of postmodern society; technology's role; critique and applicability of classical theory as related to postmodern society; inadequacies of classical theorists

■ **FORCES OF INTEGRATION AND DISINTEGRATION: SOCIETY'S JANUS FACE**
integrating and disintegrating effects of social elements; *Durkheim: The Division of Labor and Collective Conscience:* inadequacy of private contracts; meaning, maintenance, and problem of collective conscience in society; division of labor as source of morality; occupational corporate groups and solidarity; *Marx: The State, Ideology, and Capitalism:* state as employer of force and ideology; ideology as reflecting powerful interests; capitalism and stability; sources of stability as unnatural; internal sources change; *Simmel: The Web of Modern Life:* money as integrator and disintegrator; web of group affiliations; division of labor; conflict as unifier and disunifier; *Weber: Modern Society's Rational Structuring:* conflict between individual and society; interconnected rational actions and integration; forms of authority and stratification as organizers of society and sources of conflict and change

INTRODUCTION

Two valuable assets of the classical theorists are that they had a clear sense and knowledge of history and they saw society as a whole. Together, these afforded them a panoramic, big-picture view of society as it exists on the long stretch of history. Viewing the individual, groups, and society in historical context is one of the core characteristics of classical social theory. The architects of such theory presented coherent images of modern Western society, where it came from and where it was going. For them, this society had features that distinguished it from earlier societies. In addition to creating a peculiar organization for society, these features were seen as having important effects on individual personality and behavior. Some create a potential for unifying while others seemingly promote division in society. Some speed the development of unique, separated individuals while others effectively help to knit individuals together. The characteristics of modern Western society and the sources of **integration** and disintegration of society is the theme of this chapter.

What did these theorists see as the central features of modern Western society, and how do these elements differ from those frequently suggested today as characteristic of postmodern society? Can postmodern characteristics be understood using the ideas of these modernist thinkers? Let us pursue these questions.

MODERN WESTERN SOCIETY

Above all, in the view of classical theorists, modern Western society[1] is an *urban industrial* society with the following characteristics:

1. A complex division of free labor and advanced technology
2. Large, increasingly centralized economic organizations
3. Extensive urbanization

Modern Western society is also a *rational* and *rationalized* society with these essential features:

4. Bureaucratization
5. Money exchange
6. A formally organized and centralized political state
7. Secularization
8. Objective culture
9. Science

Running as a central theme through the rational elements of modern society is a focus on calculation, efficiency, and impersonality. Finally, modern Western society is viewed as an *individualizing* society characterized by the following features:

10. A preoccupation with and accelerated growth of unique individual personalities
11. Distance and alienation between individuals
12. Social, cultural, and economic heterogeneity

For the classical theorists, industrialism, rationalism, and individualism capture much of the essence of the modern lifestyle.

Society as Industrial, Urban, and Centralized

The meaning of these 12 features and their impact on the individual and society varied for Marx, Durkheim, Weber, and Simmel. For example, Marx viewed the division of labor in modern capitalist society as a source of alienation and exploitation. Division of labor, he believed, basically took whole individuals and broke them up into specialized parts so that capitalism could function effectively and profitably as one large economic machine made up of human interrelated parts. When such cleavages exist in society, "man's own act becomes an alien power opposed to him, which enslaves him instead of being controlled by him. For as soon as the division of labor begins, each man has a particular, exclusive sphere of activity, which is forced upon him and from which he cannot escape."[2] Within and because of the division of labor, individuals are not free to develop fully all their talents or to express the many sides of their natures. Needless to say, Marx's is not a rosy picture of the division of labor.

Simmel was also concerned with the splintering effects of the division of labor on human personalities, and felt that these effects were becoming more pronounced with the passage of time. "The modern division of labor permits the number of dependencies to increase just as it causes personalities to disappear behind their functions, because only one side of them operates, at the expense of all those others whose composition would make up a personality."[3] One's needs then become satisfied not because of the full exercise of all of one's abilities, but because of the various interdependencies that are created with others. The alienation suggested by Marx that results from the division of labor is echoed in Simmel: "Whenever our energies do not produce something whole as a reflection of the total personality, then the proper relationship between subject and object is

missing. ... As a result, the inadequacy that develops between the worker's exis-
tential form and that of his product because of greater specialization easily serves
to completely divorce the product from the labourer."[4] So, in Simmel's view, a
specialized division of labor creates interdependencies and allows the development of a wide range of consumption goods, but it also alienates the individual.

In sharp contrast to Marx's gloomy view and Simmel's more mixed perspective, Durkheim saw the modern, complex division of labor in a positive
light, as a means for accomplishing modern society's tasks, a way to connect
diverse individuals and groups, and an avenue for the development of unique
personalities. More specifically, Durkheim felt that as society grows and
becomes more complex, so do the problems it faces, and so does the possibility
of it becoming unwieldy and splintered. Since the specialization associated with
the division of labor means that individuals carry out distinctive yet interrelated
tasks, it also means that individuals are tied to each other because of the interdependence of their tasks. For Durkheim, this is a fundamental basis of unity in
modern society. Specialization also allows individuals to intensively develop a
particular talent. Unlike Marx, Durkheim did not see this as harmful to individuals; nor did he view the general development of many abilities as being any
better:

> Why would a more extensive activity, but more dispersed, be superior to a more
> concentrated, but circumscribed, activity? Why would there be more dignity in
> being complete and mediocre, rather than in living a more specialized, but more
> intense life, particularly if it is thus possible for us to find what we have lost in this
> specialization, through our association with other beings who have what we lack
> and who complete us?[5]

The implications of the division of labor for unity and disunity distinctly
vary among these thinkers. Clearly, the dilemmas inherent in specialization have
surfaced in recent years and in a variety of ways. In the field of medicine, specialization has proceeded apace, but there has also been a backlash reflected in
the rising popularity of holistic medicine and family practice. Should we treat the
whole person or only the diseased part? Should we emphasize physicians who are
more like "jacks-of-all-trades" and know a little about a lot of the person or
"soulless specialists" who know a lot about a little of the person? Similarly in
academia, there are long-standing issues surrounding disciplinary-based departments' fights to keep their core specialized offerings in the face of increased pressure for interdisciplinary programs and courses. As noted earlier, the division of
labor is only one part of the industrial character of modern society, but it is one
which clearly raises issues of unity and division.

Alongside the growth in the division of labor, Marx saw an increase in the size of economic organizations and an increase in the centralization of power in the economy. Due to problems inherent in its natural development, Marx concluded that eventually a relatively small number of privately owned corporations would dominate and most of us would be employees working for them. Weber also understood the exploitative tendencies of life under capitalism. Indeed, recent statistics bear witness to the immense centralization of power in the U.S. economy. Only 100 of the 200,000 U.S. industrial corporations control almost 75 percent of all U.S. industrial assets. High degrees of concentration also exist in the communications, utilities, financial, and insurance fields.[6]

Following its defining economic characteristics, extensive urbanization is another hallmark of modern society. Marx believed that the division of labor encourages the separation of town and country and the opposition of their interests. For Simmel, the city is the center of modern society and culture. It is the "seat of the money economy" and the nexus for fleeting, specialized interactions between a bewildering variety of strangers. Having spent most of his life in Berlin, Simmel was both attracted by and wary of the metropolis and its effects on individuals. City life liberates the individual and fosters the development of unique personalities at the same time that it encourages the development of a blasé attitude and alienation from others. Its effects, for Simmel, are both positive and negative. I will have more to say about the specific effects of the industrial and urban characteristics of our society in the following chapters.

Society as Rational

The great cities of modern society are homes to large bureaucracies and money exchange. Like cities, bureaucracies and money promote an impersonal and instrumental approach to others. Weber linked the rise and domination of bureaucracies in modern society to the growing administrative problems accompanying increasing complexity and to the rise of a money economy. Weber believed that bureaucracies have machinelike efficiency and, as such, are superior in effectiveness to other forms of organization, but are also instruments of great power for whoever controls them. And once created, they are almost impossible to dismantle. One has only to think of the many recent presidents who have promised to cut down state bureaucracy only to have it grow once again. Bureaucracies also reinforce the impersonality of modern life and magnify the distance between the individual and the state.

Like Weber, Durkheim also was convinced that the state would increase in size and complexity, but he did not view it with the same negative cast as Weber. Instead of seeing the state as some impassive, remote bureaucracy, Durkheim interpreted the state as a necessary preserver of the rights of individuals. It is there to protect the individual and ensure that there is an environment hospitable to the flowering of individual talents and proclivities. Thus, instead of crushing individuals, the state promotes their freedom.

For Marx, in sharp contrast, the state's structure and policies directly reflect the exploitative relationship that characterizes the tie between capitalists and workers. Consequently, the state is an instrument of oppression that promotes the interests of capitalists against those of workers. Political power reflects economic power: "The executive of the modern State is but a committee for managing the common affairs of the whole bourgeoisie."[7] Today, we see an incredible influx of money into political campaigns and in the legislative process. Members of Congress pay lip service to the need for campaign reform, yet they delay and drag their feet when it comes to putting their policies where their mouths are. The state as an impersonal entity dominated by individuals with personal interests continues to be a subject of deep controversy.

In addition to a money economy and a powerful organized state, objective culture, secularization, and science further reinforce the rational character of modern society. Simmel defined *objective culture* as those human products and objects that take on a power and life of their own far removed from the creative human impulse that originally gave rise to them. **Objective culture** is exemplified in hardened, rigid schools of thought and art that originally were the vibrant ideas of individuals, but now have their own fixed autonomous existence. It stands as a separate entity that confines and restricts **subjective culture** (human creativity). Objective culture can be found most readily in the city, where cultural artifacts reside. Like other characteristics of modern society, objective culture imprints an impersonal character on the modern lifestyle.

Secularization is a theme found in the work of all classical theorists. But again, their interpretations of its implications differ. Durkheim, Marx, and Weber each believed that science and its increasing influence would have a dampening effect on traditional religions. Much of this belief reflects the Enlightenment's tenets regarding the power of reason in human beings and the faith in science as twin guides to social progress. As science explains more and more of reality, religion's function in this area diminishes, according to Durkheim. Science advances slowly, however; thus, there will be a speculative role for religion indefinitely. The sacred element in social life—faith, cults, rituals—is eternal. Indeed, as societies come into greater contact with each other, Durkheim thought that a universal civil religion may be the primary mechanism by which all humans could unite.[8] Some have argued that, alongside science, a strengthening of religion is needed in modern life, because each can provide answers to questions that the other cannot: "These modes of experience aren't contradictory. Though they come from separate universes of discourse, a person can hold them all in an integrated personality and not be schizophrenic."[9]

In contrast to this conclusion and to Durkheim's view, Marx believed that religion would gradually fade away as a force in social life as individuals became fully and accurately conscious of their situations. The need for religion as a palliative would decline in strength as capitalism developed according to its inexorable logic, and would eventually disappear in future societies. Given the revival of religious fundamentalism in the United States and the overwhelming percentage of individuals who believe in God today, Marx's perspective on this issue would appear to be less accurate than Durkheim's. However, the less obvious otherworldliness and rise of some religions as large-monied businesses, such as Scientology, would appear to reinforce the importance of Marx's materialist capitalist view of modern institutions.

Weber also believed that materialism was a realistic prospect for modern society. He thought that the religious roots of the Protestant ethic as a motivator for economic action by individuals would become secularized as mature capitalism established itself in Western society. The power of wealth and the rules of capitalistic behavior would displace the religious ethic. In modern society, ethics and morality have a rational rather than religious basis. According to Weber, the lack of concern for material objects, which characterizes the religious person, is rapidly disappearing in modern capitalistic society: "Material goods have gained an increasing and finally an inexorable power over the lives of men as at no previous period in history."[10] In fact, wealth and its pursuit create a burden that weighs heavily on individuals and directs their lives. In this regard, Weber's depiction and prediction is telling and worth quoting fully:

> In the field of its highest development, in the United States, the pursuit of wealth, stripped of its religious and ethical meaning, tends to become associated with purely mundane passions, which often actually give it the character of sport. No one knows who will live in this cage of the future, or whether at the end of this tremendous development entirely new prophets will arise, or there will be a great rebirth of old ideas and ideals, or, if neither, mechanized petrification, embellished with a sort of compulsive self-importance. For of the last stage of this cultural development, it might well be truly said: "Specialists without spirit, sensualists without heart; this nullity imagines that it has attained a level of civilization never before achieved."[11]

Harsh words, indeed. But reactions by many in the United States against crass materialism, selfish individualism, the perceived absence of fundamental principles and values, and the "rebirth" of religious fundamentalism suggest that Weber was on to something when he wrote these words. The pervasive impact of wealth on our lives will be explored in several later chapters. In the view of these thinkers, although pockets of narrow religiosity might persevere, modern society as a whole has increasingly become a secular and narrowly rational society.

Society as Individualistic

In addition to its industrial and rational character, the centrality of the individual in modern Western society is a third overriding theme. Weber's reference in the preceding quote to "compulsive self-importance" implies some of his concern about the individual. Marx had other worries, however. He argued that both capitalists and workers live an alienated life under capitalism, but he also felt that the unity of humans with nature and their own natures would be restored in **communist society.** Individuals struggle to be free and to direct their own lives and develop themselves fully. Since private property alienates individuals, its abolition under communism would eliminate human alienation. For Durkheim, egoism grows as society becomes more specialized and industrialized. But to be happy, feel free, and be in control of their own destinies, individuals need guidance and must be sensitive to others. The alternative is chaos, confusion, and constant irritation. The **moral individualism** Durkheim envisioned in modern society is not to be confused with selfish, egoistic individualism. Rather, he thought that individualism, in its more enlightened state, would develop as societies expand and intermingle with others across the world. Traditional and ethnocentric barriers would fall as humans begin to realize that we are all part of a common humanity. "And since each of us incarnates something of humanity, each individual consciousness contains something divine and thus finds itself marked with a character which renders it sacred and inviolable to others. Therein lies all individualism."[12] In effect, Durkheim surmised that individualism will become a religious ethic that unites all humanity. The social and cultural heterogeneity of modern society make individualism more likely and moral individualism more necessary. However, the intransigience of group prejudice would suggest that we have not reached the humaneness in the United States that Durkheim projected for modern society.

Both Weber and Simmel also considered individualism a core part of modern society, but their interpretations are quite different from Durkheim's. For them, it is the rational, calculating individual that is a predominant feature of modern life. Individuals who weigh the pros and cons for themselves and who are self-interested are the prototypes of the modern citizen. As society grows, and cities become larger and denser, individuals move around as disinterested strangers pursuing their own lives, living in their own private cocoons, parts of their lives barely overlapping with those of others. Although appearing to be free,

Weber believed that capitalism and bureaucracy are forces that continue to dominate individuals in modern society. For Simmel, it is money as a form of exchange and the demands of city life that leave their imprint on the human psyche. Certainly, the nature of individualism, of our ties to others, and of our responsibility to our society are issues that are at the forefront of debates today about welfare, abortion, civic duty, and many others. The issue of the relationship between the individual and community will be taken up in the next chapter.

THE POSTMODERN ELEMENT

As all of the preceding attests, the complex modern society envisioned by the classical theorists is a society marked by urbanism and industrialism, technological progress, rationality, and individualism. It is a society in which economic, political, and scientific institutions play central roles. Finally, it is a society that does not fully or explicitly take into account the following postmodern, late-capitalist traits that so many academics have recently said are dominant in our society:

- The proliferation and rapid changing of images
- The superficiality or flatness of everyday life
- Constant change and little stability or fixity of structures
- The breakdown of inner and outer boundaries
- The globalization of economies
- The replacement of truth with multiple voices and relativism
- The blurring/merging of reality and simulations

All of this suggests that modern society—which our four classical theorists viewed as being characterized by certainty, clarity, predictability, and firm structure—is being replaced by a postmodern society in which uncertainty, relativity, flux, and disintegration are prominent. Many of these conditions have been brought about by revolutions in technology (e.g., computers and media), while others have been instigated primarily by accelerations in the multiplicity and growing power of varied groups and subcultures in our society. Information technology has made communication possible between individuals around the globe and has made knowledge and information accessible to anyone who can afford it. The result has been an unceasing bombardment and proliferation of data from all kinds of divergent groups; the breakdown of national, cultural, and economic boundaries; and the dissolution of barriers between public and private arenas, work and home. The long arm of technology has reached everywhere, from the most remote to the most private places.

Media technology has also progressed exponentially to the point of creating multiple virtual realities that take on lives of their own. Disneyworld is a real place but at the same time it represents something that is unreal. Whole worlds are invented through simulations into which individuals can transport themselves, further blurring the line between image and reality. The louder sound of multiple voices from an increasing number of subcultures and segments of society makes notions of underlying commonality more suspect. What is "true" varies and what appears "taken for granted" becomes problematic. The firm bedding on which we thought we were standing moves under our feet.

The movie *Wag the Dog* illustrates the postmodern theme of how sophisticated technology and the media can combine to create a "fictitious reality" out of a set of images, which is then believed by those viewing it to be something that is objectively real. In the storyline, a spin doctor and a Hollywood producer combine their talents to create a fictitious war between the United States and Albania to divert attention from some real problems the U.S. president is experiencing at home. A series of press releases, script writing, and manufactured TV images are used to convince people that a war is actually occurring when it really is not. (If you see it reported on TV, it must be real, right?) The line between the manufactured and the real is effectively blurred. One piece of anecdotal evidence for this virtual reality is the increasing use of real journalists in Hollywood films. This is a divergence from the heretofore standard practice "of separating network news from Hollywood make-believe."[13]

The proponents of the postmodern view of society argue that since society has changed so dramatically, the "grand narratives" of traditional theorists no longer apply. Obviously, I do not agree. Although some of the specifics of contemporary society (e.g., the computer revolution) may not have been fully anticipated by the classical social theorists, most of the characteristics of modern society to which they sensitized us still continue, and many of the postmodern traits of current society can still be understood within classical frameworks. For example, Marx's theory of the capitalist process and capitalism's evolution can still help us understand the globalization of economies and the advancement of technology. Information technology's expanding reach is still often to find new customers, new markets, and new outposts for capitalist interests. The bottom line of many simulated adventures is still profit.

As to the bewildering array of images and the rapidity of their change, Simmel was attuned to the rapid changes in metropolitan centers that money exchange allows, fashion permits, and striving for individuality seeks. In many ways, the urbane Simmel's ideas lend themselves very well to the postmodern turn of mind.[14] Moreover, Durkheim's focus on the significance of cults, rituals, symbols, morality—in short, the cultural elements of society—together with his discussions of individualization and anomie, fit very well into analyses of images and change in postmodern society.[15] The persistence of the religious element in society would not have come as a surprise to Durkheim. Finally, Weber's concerns for status groups and sources of domination in modern society can help us understand current pressures for groups to split off and lead their own lifestyles, as well as the manipulation and intrusion into private lives by sophisticated marketers and distant bureaucracies. As it is for many poststructuralist and postmodern thinkers, power was a prominent theme in Weber's work.

All this said, it does not mean that there are no problems in applying the ideas of these men to an understanding of contemporary society. On the contrary, there are areas where some of the classical theorists had either little to say or were off the mark in their predictions. Marx clearly underestimated the ability of capitalism to manipulate and buy off workers, and he did not appear to anticipate all the incredible advances in communication technologies. He also paid less attention to the cultural component of social life that appears to be so prominent in social science today. Nor does present society appear to be as rigid, bleak, or grey as Weber may have anticipated. Large bureaucratic organizations certainly fill our economic and political landscapes, but smaller, newer businesses continually crop up, making for a more vibrant society. And religion has certainly not become secularized, as recent years have seen the growth of evangelical and fundamentalist religious groups. Amidst the daily and seemingly inescapable assault of conflicting opinions and discourses, Weber's own dying words—"The real thing is Truth"—appear to be quaint at best, words spoken in a simpler, more certain time.[16]

Finally, because of their focus on urban life, none of these theorists appeared to place much importance on rural life or the environment, with the possible exception of Marx's concern for humans working with and wresting their living from nature while at the same time being a part of nature. Recent public worries about a polluted environment and a desire to create green spaces and maintain the sanctity of rural places were not predicted by these theorists. Still, as has been shown, they had much to say that still informs our thinking about current issues, perhaps most notably processes that divide and unite us.

FORCES OF INTEGRATION AND DISINTEGRATION: SOCIETY'S JANUS FACE

It has been said many times that the classical theorists were concerned with issues of order and change, structure and process, integration and disintegration. These twin themes underline the theorists' attempts to understand what holds societies together and what tears them apart. Following Simmel, it is in the outcome of the creative tension between these conflicting processes that societies receive their shape. Many of the societal elements that promote integration or cohesiveness also are sources of division and conflict. The very forces that bring together some members of society drive others away. Like the ancient Roman god, Janus, society faces in two directions—one toward the outside and the other toward the inside.

Durkheim: The Division of Labor and Collective Conscience

Durkheim, especially, was concerned with issues of social integration and disintegration, and explicitly said a great deal about them. Indeed, he is said to have had "a rage for order and unity in the body social."[17]

Durkheim argued that there are several potential sources of integration in society. Among these are the (1) collective conscience/consciousness, (2) division of labor, and (3) corporate groups. Durkheim did not believe that individual contracts were a major source of societal integration because such contracts, he felt, involve only specific, transient private interests, and assume an initial degree of conflict between the parties involved. Self-interest, no matter how enlightened, is not enough to bind us together. Rather, it is the laws and customs that undergird and lie behind such contracts and that are part of the collective conscience that encourages equity and solidarity in such relationships. Such forces are even more necessary as contracts proliferate across a large population.

Collective conscience refers to the underlying, common beliefs and values that exist independent of particular individuals and across generations, and that tie a society together. It is "the totality of beliefs and sentiments common to average citizens of the same society"; it "has its own life," is "diffuse in every reach of society," and is strongest when personified in and exercised "through the medium of a defined organ."[18] These properties of continuity, pervasiveness, and personification make the collective conscience a potentially powerful source of morality, of direction and conformity for members of a society. Periodic rituals and ceremonies, such as Fourth of July celebrations, help keep common cultural beliefs about the United States vibrant and alive. This is also true of **totemic symbols,** such as the flag. The fact that in 1997 the U.S. Congress considered a constitutional amendment to outlaw the burning of the flag provides an indication of the importance of the flag as a part of our collective conscience. However, in large, heterogeneous, complex, rapidly changing societies such as the United States, the breadth and depth of the collective conscience are not as great as in smaller, less changeful societies. Consequently, collective conscience in modern societies such as the United States is not as overpowering or evident.

Durkheim's notion of the collective conscience raises a question for us: What do we have in common, if anything? The perception of a lack of common traditional values such as respect, honesty, hard work, and so on is brought up often by those who work with youth. A teacher at an Ohio school recently asked his students what they would do if an automatic teller machine (ATM) gave them $200 instead of the $20 for which they asked. "All of them said they'd keep the money. . . . The kids know it's wrong, but their world is situational ethics. . . . Will I get away with it?"[19] Also brought up were the feelings on the part of students that it is okay to cheat, even if it is wrong, because everyone is doing it. Even though the students have values, they are not well developed, the teacher remarked, because "no one is pushing them to do the right thing."[20] How do we instill values that bind us to the community without suffocating the individual? Is it possible to come together based on what we have in common and yet still maintain our desired identities as individuals and separate groups? Durkheim argued that a unifying unselfish morality and individualism could and would coexist in modern society.[21]

Clearly, this issue of commonality is a critical issue to address when considering what it is that can bind us together as a nation and as a world. In the absence of a broad, binding moral framework as a set of guidelines, Durkheim felt that individuals lose their sense of direction in life. Life becomes meaningless. There is neither a moral base or anchor with which to gauge one's behavior nor a specific, firm end-goal for one to seek. Anything goes and goes anywhere. In this state of anomie, as Durkheim called it, integration is threatened. Anomie is a disintegrating force and is especially likely to occur when society is in a state of rapid change, when old morals have evaporated but new ones have not yet replaced them.

In addition to the collective conscience, Durkheim cited the *division of labor* in modern society as a basis for solidarity. In any industrial society, the occupational order is a central part of its social structure. Because an intricate division of labor creates interdependencies among positions and individuals, it is one means by which individuals and groups are knitted together in modern societies. The awareness and consideration of others required by the division of labor makes it a moral phenomenon because it curbs the selfish, egoistic tendencies of individuals. In essence, "the division of labor becomes the chief source of social solidarity, [and] at the same time, the foundation of the moral order."[22] For Durkheim, as industrialization advances, the division of labor "resolves this apparent antinomy" between persons becoming "at once more individual and more solidary."[23] Unrestrained egoism is a threat to an integrated society. Individualism must always be tempered by an awareness of one's ties and obligations to others if society is to avoid flying apart. As in the case of anomie, excessive egoism signals a morbid lack of integration in society, which can translate into higher suicide rates.[24] I will examine the case of egoistic suicide more fully in Chapter 3.

A final source of integration discussed by Durkheim is **corporate groups.** This source is closely tied to Durkheim's discussion of the division of labor, since corporate groups are occupationally based. The division of labor is a source of solidarity because it is based on *differences*. In contrast, corporate groups tie together individuals who are occupationally *similar*. Because of the complexity of the division of labor, each industry must organize its members to develop the rules and ethics by which it operates. These rules define the duties of occupations and their prescribed relationships with other occupations. As such, they weaken egoism and the chances of misdirection. The state itself cannot regulate occupations because there are too many of them, and the state is not equipped to handle such a large task. Besides, argued Durkheim, because they are in size intermediate between individuals and the state, corporate groups serve as a more effective means to "penetrate deeply into individual consciences and socialize them within."[25] Corporate groups bring individuals more effectively into the life of a whole society, and therefore function as a linchpin, tying groups and the society together.

Marx: The State, Ideology, and Capitalism

Marx's view of what holds modern societies such as the United States together is markedly different from Durkheim's perspective. First of all, Marx was principally and more narrowly concerned with *capitalist* society, whereas Durkheim focused on the evolution of *industrial* societies in general. Moreover, Durkheim emphasized the positive, functional, national effects of the mechanisms of integration, whereas Marx emphasized the roles of state force, ideology, and the capitalist system itself in ensuring stability and continuity in society.

As a political instrument of the capitalist class, the *state* develops laws that serve the interests of that class, and provides a legal system and military force to ensure that these laws are obeyed. "Each step in the development of the bourgeoisie was accompanied by a corresponding political advance of that class.... [T]he bourgeoisie has at last, since the establishment of Modern Industry and of the world-market, conquered for itself, in the modern representative State, exclusive political sway."[26] The state relies on a stable economy for its revenue, whereas economic powers depend on the state for protection of their interests. This handmaiden relationship compels the state to promote structural stability. As a political and ideological tool, the state can use its vast power for the development of policies and interpretations of social-economic situations that are sympathetic to capitalist business. Behind the pressures for widespread obedience to laws lies the threat of punishment for those who disobey. The state is the sole employer of the legitimate means of force in society.

In addition to the state, *ideologies* that reflect the interests of those with economic power are used to justify laws and existing social-structural arrangements. Like all ideas or mental phenomena, ideologies mirror conditions and relationships in the socioeconomic structure of a society: "The ideas of the ruling class are, in every age, the ruling ideas: i.e. the class which is the dominant material force in society is at the same time its dominant *intellectual* force."[27] Education and religion play prominent roles in this area, since they socialize us to become good citizens and play by the rules. Schools encourage civic responsibility (read "obedience"), fitting in, and playing one's part in the existing economy; and religion, like an opiate, calms people, putting them to sleep and keeping them unaware of their own exploitation.

As intellectuals, economists, in particular, are seen by Marx as reinforcing beliefs in capitalist economic arrangements. They do this by suggesting that relationships in the market economy of supply and demand are consistent with nature and therefore follow natural laws, rather than being artificially created. If they are "natural," how can one object to them or why would one wish to change them? Because of the powerful effect of the economic institution on the rest of society, the logic of market ideologies, which consider monetary costs and benefits in weighing the relative values of commodities, become increasingly applied to all aspects of life, even human "commodities."[28] (See Chapter 6.)

Finally, according to Marx, the *nature of the capitalist system* (1) creates interdependencies between individuals and (2) keeps the minds of individuals on their everyday routines. These effects optimize the chances for continuation of the system and minimize the probability that significant change will be initiated. First, individuals are tied together by economic links, by the need for wages or profit. There is a cash nexus. Second, when enmeshed day after day in the work of one's *alienating* job, it is difficult to take the time and energy, yet alone to have the perspective, to see how things could be changed for the betterment of everyone. It is difficult to rise above one's immediate situation and see the big picture in context. In this way, capitalism itself promotes a kind of inertia that keeps existing economic arrangements intact.

To Marx, the sources of integration within capitalism are not natural bases of unity. Although they make up a large part of the social and economic structure, they are unnatural and consequently are also sources of strain, divisiveness, and dissolution. Marx's dialectical approach is evident here; the social structure contains within it the seeds of its own destruction. Marx saw nothing wrong with technology itself; indeed, he viewed it as a means by which humans could be released from much of the drudgery of daily life. The effects of technology on the quality of human life appear to be mixed, and will be discussed primarily in Chapters 3 and 6.[29]

Unfortunately, although technology and the means of production within capitalist society have progressed, social and property relationships within the economic structure remain the same. Alienation and class structure, and the private property upon which the latter is based, persist. This constitutes an internal contradiction causing change to occur, ultimately leading to what Marx felt would be a better society. In sum, the means of integration are also sources of disintegration, and disintegration leads to a new and more human means of integration. It is only in the future society of communism that Marx believed more fundamental and harmonious unity would be established. Humans would work together and each could vary their tasks to fit the development of all their talents. In this context, humanity and nature would work in harmony. What stands in the way of this natural unity is capitalism with its private property, class structure, and alienating labor. We need to keep Marx's perspective on these matters in mind when addressing the treatment of humans as commodities and growing inequality in later chapters. I will explore the adequacy of Marx's view of capitalism more fully in Chapter 7.

Simmel: The Web of Modern Life

Simmel had a more optimistic view of capitalism than Marx, and preferred its competition and private market approach to what he thought were the individual-stunting greyness and dominating qualities of socialism and communism. Perhaps the most intriguing aspect of Simmel's sociology is his dialectical treatment of so many components of modern urban life. As in Marx, many of the same factors that Simmel sees as central in contemporary society have both integrating and disintegrating social effects. Among the most important of these factors are money, group affiliations, division of labor, and conflict.

Modern capitalist societies such as the United States operate effectively, in part, because the use of *money as a medium of exchange* brings together all kinds of people and at the same time provides the individual with increased freedom of choice. Since money is a universal means of exchange, it can move easily between objects and services without regard to their differences in quality. Money is the standard measure by which to evaluate objects, humans, and services. In a manner of speaking, *everything* has its price. Simmel argued that the values placed on each object and the money values that define the relationship between objects creates an objective web of relationships that exists independently of individuals.[30] In effect, an extensive buyer and seller network is established.

The *web of group affiliations* in modern life is also a fundamental basis for its integration. Social ties based on fixed criteria such as common kinship, location, and biology were more prominent in earlier societies; ties within modern society are more likely to be based on individuals having similar interests, educations, or occupations. Simmel associates the latter bases for affiliation with greater individual freedom because choice is involved in selecting group membership. In contrast, one has little choice about blood ties or biological makeup.

The shift in the bases of group affiliation to those of interests and occupation is one source of the greater freedom of individuals in modern society. Individuals belong to different sets of groups, some of which have overlapping interests or individual memberships and others of which do not. This builds and reinforces the uniqueness of each person. So while networks of overlapping groups tie individuals to society, they also promote the individuality and separation from others of each person.

The size of the group also affects the means by which it can be integrated. In small groups, socialism, a rigid normative framework, and immediate surveillance of members can bind individuals together, but in large groups, a division of labor is needed: "A very large number of people can constitute a unit only if there is a complex division of labor."[31] What would be a source of cohesion in a small group would endanger a larger one, and vice versa. The *division of labor* provides an abstract, impersonal basis for association in contemporary society. The interlocking and coordination of individuals and groups in cities is also supported by a reliance on the clock—strict schedules, work shifts, appointment times, and so on.

Simmel's dialectical perspective, the joining of positive and negative elements in social life, is continued in his arguments about *conflict*. Although ostensibly a divisive force, conflict can also be a source of integration in that it is a means to resolve problems and reach some kind of accommodation or unity. Conversely, closeness and tight integration, although sources of unity, can be causes of enmity and jealousy, which, in turn, can provoke conflict. Opposition and harmony are tethered together in social life. As noted earlier, the unity of any social structure is an inextricable blend of both harmonious and conflicting elements: "Relations of conflict do not by themselves produce a social structure, but only in cooperation with unifying forces. Only both together constitute the group as a concrete, living unit."[32] Conflict is needed for life and growth of the individual as well as society. Clearly, Simmel does not treat conflict as a negative force in society. Opposition often makes life bearable, is a source of satisfaction, is part of a full life, and can even strengthen and save a relationship.

Weber: Modern Society's Rational Structuring

Like Simmel but unlike Marx, Weber did not imagine a modern society in which conflict and opposition could be absent. The growing rationalization and bureaucratization of life means that there is always a conflict between the individual and society's structure, since individuals will either be dominated by an "iron cage" or seek to escape through charismatic movements or other religious avenues.

Weber's view of the organization of contemporary society begins with the intersection of the individual and society. Modern individuals, especially, engage in rational social action, in that behavior is viewed as a means to an end, and means are chosen according to their effectiveness and efficiency in reaching the desired end. For example, let us say that a person has set "money" as the end to be sought. If money is the end (and a means to other valued ends), that person has to select the best means to reach the goal of money. If we multiply this situation, realizing that each individual is engaged in many such social actions, and that all individuals do this, resulting in many intersections between individuals, we obtain an image of society which, in part, is tied together by individuals engaging in *interconnected social actions*. This is one source of integration.

Many of these social actions take place within the context of large, formally structured organizations, which increasingly dominate modern society. Rational-legal authority (i.e., obedience to others based on their formal positions in organizations) is a basis for stability and integration in society. Relationships and social orders can also be "legitimated" or justified on the basis of tradition or charisma. Individuals willingly obey and tolerate a given arrangement in society because it may be based on tradition, (i.e., this is the way things always have been done). When traditions are attacked or weakened, tradition can no longer justify the existing social order. In a pluralistic, changing society like the United States, this is especially likely. Finally, relationships and social orders can also be legitimated through belief in the charisma of a leader. Such a foundation is most likely to appear when the existing society is in a state of disarray or crisis. The leader offers something fresh—a solution or the promise of a new order. In this sense, charisma is antitraditional and even revolutionary. But since it is dependent on the personality of a given leader, it is also fragile and must be **routinized** into an institution so that the ideas and relationships can continue long after the original leader has died.

The structure of a society also contains stratification along class, status, and **party** lines, which further organizes it and creates positions for individuals within it. Since modern capitalism is an advanced industrial, rapidly changing society, Weber felt that economic class position, or market situation, is the most significant of these positions. Social status position, based on an estimation of honor or prestige, is more prominent in more static traditional situations, but also operates in modern society. One's party or organized political power further structures society and one's place in it, and can be based on one's class and/or status.

In sum, social actions, bureaucracy, bases of legitimacy, and multidimensional social stratification all help to integrate contemporary society. However, Weber realized that relationships and social orders can also be defined as illegitimate as conditions change, that bureaucracies are tools of power that can alienate average citizens, that capitalism and class are often bases of exploitation as well as integration, and that inconsistencies can occur between economic, social, and political orders. Thus, the bases of integration can also provide the seeds for potential conflict and change in society.

CONCLUSION

Each of our theorists recognized modern society as urban, industrial, rational, and individualistic, and also recognized its tendencies toward both integration and disintegration. Society has forces within it that propel it in both directions, and often the same factors have potential for both effects simultaneously. Centrifugal forces create change but may also threaten to pull society apart, whereas centripetal forces foster internal unity but may also engender undue rigidity and conformity. Society is pulled in both directions, and its final shape reflects this fundamental tension and contradiction.

Contemporary U.S. society expresses its contradictory nature in a variety of ways. Americans extol individual freedom, yet at the same time people are at the mercy of economic, political, and social forces beyond their control. We appear to direct our lives, yet we are controlled. The individual seeks autonomy, but society demands allegiance and conformity. We often are committed to ourselves, but show little commitment to society. Modern civilization has given us the "cult of the individual," but we also treat individuals as commodities. We have a high standard of living as a nation, yet our lives and our nation seem, in the view of many, to have lost their moral basis. Many own more things, but for them life often has less meaning. Our society is rife with large hierarchical formal organizations and status distinctions, while at the same time we give voice to our love of equality. We, like all industrial societies, are a nation of contradictions, of elements that bring us together and force us apart.

Many of the contradictions in society play themselves out in the intersection of the individual and the larger community. Our obligations to and desires for ourselves often seem to get in the way of the demands from and our obligations to society. The two would seem to pull us in opposite directions. The classical theorists generally did not feel that this had to be the case, nor did they always feel that this conflict was negative, and most suggested means by which the individual and society could be integrated for the benefit of both. Some of these theorists also suggested that the conflict between the social and the personal is reflected in the dichotomous nature of human beings. All of us, they suggested, are both angels and animals. Just as society has two faces, we have two sides to our nature. As we will see in the next chapter, the relationships between them can be accommodating and even harmonious, or they can be hostile and divisive.

QUESTIONS TO PONDER

1. Postmodern theorists often suggest that rapid changes in technology (e.g., computers, communication networks, media techniques) have basically altered society and culture. To what extent do you think this is true and to what extent do you think society and culture have remained basically the same?

2. Marx, Simmel, and others have argued that social change occurs most fundamentally from inconsistencies and conflicts within the society rather than from forces outside it. What examples can you think of that would illustrate their point?

3. Why is conflict necessary to a society? How can it actually save a social relationship? What would a society without conflict be like?

CHAPTER 3

PRIVATE LIVES AND PUBLIC CONNECTIONS

CHAPTER IN BRIEF

- **INTRODUCTION**
issue of increasing selfishness and individual/community relationship; dualistic nature of self and individual/community obligations

- **THE MEANING OF THE NATURAL SELF**
Dr. Jekyll, Mr. Hyde, and Durkheim's view of egoistic and social sides of human nature; Simmel's rational and non-rational, egoistic and sympathetic sides of human nature; Marx's view of humans as naturally social and productive; Weber's analysis of types of motivation and action, and search for meaning

- **THE INDIVIDUAL AND THE COMMUNITY: A DELICATE BALANCE**
individual exploited and alienated in capitalist society (Marx); individual controlled by large, distant social institutions (Weber); objective vs. subjective culture; individual/society conflict and growth (Simmel); individual/society balance and integration (Durkheim); excessive individualism; meaning of communitarianism

- **THE PUBLIC EYE IN THE PRIVATE LIFE**
technology's potentials; Internet access to private information; creation of relationships on web; anonymity, security, and intimacy on web (Simmel); virtual vs. physical communities (Durkheim); abuse of Internet for private gain; Internet, isolation, and community; causes of Internet and web use (Marx and Weber)

- **SEPARATION AND SUICIDE**
integration, isolation, regulation, and types of suicide (Durkheim); extent and sources of youth suicide; exploitation, economic dominance, meaninglessness, and youth suicide (Marx)

INTRODUCTION

This chapter deals with the relationship between individuals and the larger community, one which was of deep concern to classical thinkers. Recurrent claims that people have become more self-centered in recent years, less caring or sensitive to the needs of others, and alienated from governmental affairs suggest a growing rift between the individual and the community. Abundant numbers of self-help books encourage us to turn inward, to develop our own minds and bodies, and to be at peace with ourselves. Declines in charity giving, especially among the most wealthy, further suggest our lack of concern for others or social problems that seem so far away from our immediate lives. Recent emphases on individual rights and frivolous lawsuits, among other signs, suggest to many that the pendulum has swung too far away from social obligations and personal responsibility toward personal rights and obligations to self.

In his treatise on racial problems in the United States, Cornel West eloquently argues that we need to set individual ambitions aside and identify more with what all of us have in common to realize our promise as a nation.[1] He goes on to decry black leaders who are seemingly more concerned with their own careers than they are with blacks and whites as a community. A number of African American scholars such as Henry Louis Gates and William Wilson similarly view the class divisions within the black community as harmful to its development as a coherent, empathetic community. While the danger in these scenarios is most often linked to the selfishness of individuals, one must be careful not to forget that an excessively integrated community can create its own problems through its control and suffocation of the individual. The relationship between the individual and the community has always been viewed as a critical and dynamic one, with the emphasis swinging back and forth between them.

The three major issues discussed in this chapter address different emphases in this relationship. The controversy over the relative importance of individual rights and community obligations suggests the tenuous balance in this relationship; the controversy related to computer technology shows the invasion of the community into the private lives of individuals; and the controversy surrounding the causes of youth suicide demonstrates the importance of individuals being integrated into the community.

What we think the relationship between human beings and community is and should be is heavily affected by what we think human beings are like in the first place. If we see people as being basically selfish or animalistic, our view of their attachment to the community will be quite different than if we see them as being basically cooperative and social in nature. This concern over the selfish element in our natures has often led national politicians to appeal to our more social, civic, and civilized side. In his inaugural address, John F. Kennedy extorted us to "ask not what your country can do for you—ask what you can do for your country." In trying to stop the massive violence threatening the country, Abraham Lincoln asked us to listen to the "better angels" of our nature. In this chapter, we will discuss how this apparent conflict between self and society was understood by classical theorists and how it has manifested itself in contemporary issues regarding the individual's connection to society, privacy, and suicide. But first, we need to take a closer look at how these theorists viewed human nature.

THE MEANING OF THE NATURAL SELF

Part of the reason classical theorists often viewed the relationship between the individual and community as problematic is that they believed individuals possessed a dualistic nature. One side was generally presented as selfish and antisocial, whereas the other was seen as more civilized and socially oriented. Like the Janus face of society, if humans have two sides to their nature, one pulling them toward the self and the other toward society, it is no wonder that the conflict between self and society has been viewed as fundamental and ineradicable.

In the well-known classic *The Strange Case of Dr. Jekyll and Mr. Hyde,* Robert Lewis Stevenson relates the story of a man who experienced pain because of the twin but hostile sides of his nature, and who tried, unsuccessfully, to separate these sides so that each could operate independently of the other. The assumption, of course, was that if left together, each side could contaminate and cause pain for the other. The higher side is presented as being kind, intellectual, moral, and civilized, whereas the lower component is depicted as self-seeking, emotional, amoral, and uncivilized. Dr. Jekyll is "good" and "noble"; Mr. Hyde is the "lethal side," being "wholly evil." Internally, Dr. Jekyll feels a "perennial war" between these two sides of his self. He argues that "it was the curse of mankind that . . . these polar twins should be continuously struggling."[2]

There is a strong parallel here with Durkheim's perspective on the dualism of human nature. He saw individuals as having two sides to their natures: egoistic and social. The first is rooted in the biological organism of the person, whereas the second receives its characteristics from society. As in the case of Dr. Jekyll, the properties of spirituality, reason, morality, scientific thinking, and sociality are found in our social natures according to Durkheim, while as in Mr. Hyde, the animalistic, sensual, selfish, profane, and material are in the egoistic part. These two sides of our "double" nature which are "wholly opposite . . . nevertheless . . . interpenetrate in such a way as to produce the mixed and contradictory being" that is the human being.[3] Durkheim argued that as civilization advances, the war between these two segments would intensify. "All evidence compels us to expect our effort in the struggle between the two beings within us to increase with the growth of civilization."[4] As the division of labor, laws, and the state progress, so too does the civilized and social nature of human beings, as well as the deepening of the conflict between the sides of our nature. This suggests that the conflict between the *rights* and selfish desires of individuals, on the one hand, and their social *obligations* to others and the community, on the other hand, would also intensify. Thus, for Durkheim, any conflict that appears between self and society is rooted in the imbalance in development of the two sides of our human nature. Society needs to be within us to curb our selfish nature. As individuals, we need society because we need involvement with social life in order to become truly civilized.

Simmel also had a dualistic, though somewhat different, view of human nature.[5] While individuals possess rationality, intellect, and a mind, they also possess a "soul"—a nonrational dimension. The latter is associated with the emotions, love, faith, and aesthetics, and is a core part of our human nature. In contemporary society, it is this subjective part of our humanity that is stifled, while the objective, rational, intellectual part flourishes. This is demonstrated in the large metropolis, the quintessential representation of modern society, where the head dominates over the heart. In the city, the objective character of the money economy and division of labor has nurtured our rationality but not our nonrationality. But since both are important parts of our selves, both must develop and be in rough balance. Human nature also contains a combination of two motivations: egoistic hostility as well as sympathy toward others. Individuals have parallel needs to separate themselves from others as distinctive beings but also to share a fellow-feeling with them. The identity and unity of both the self and society are forged out of their conflict with each other. So, paradoxically, conflict between individuals and society is inevitable but necessary as each tries to establish its own identity and integrity.

For Marx, the confrontation between the individual and capitalist society is not one that can be looked on favorably. Marx saw humans as being naturally creative, proactive, social, and in harmony with nature. Productive activity/labor is naturally fulfilling to individuals. They desire to be engaged in meaningful work in which they think *and* act. They do not shun it because it is through such work that individuals realize their true potential. Individuals have many abilities and desire freedom to develop them. Finally, and most important, human nature is also social in character since humans' "own existence is a social activity." We are conscious of our basic similarity to others—that is, our **species-being.** Much of what we become, however, is determined by our relationships in society: "The real nature of man is the totality of social relations."[6] There is no *inherent* conflict between the individual and society; it is the manner in which society is organized that creates problems in the relationship between individuals and society. Capitalist society hinders the full expression of human nature. As such, capitalist society creates individuals who are alienated from their own natures.

In contrast to Durkheim, Marx, and Simmel, Weber theorized that there is no strong component of internal opposition between parts of human nature or personality. Individuals try to make sense of their lives, to give them meaning, and can engage in different kinds of actions to do so.[7] He distinguished between **rational action, affective action,** and **traditional action,** in which behavior is motivated by the intellect, emotions, or tradition, respectively. Weber felt that purposively rational action, in which one carefully assesses the pros and cons of courses of action and their consequences, was becoming dominant in modern society. The search for meaning in life and the source of its meaning are important issues for Weber, and are reflected in his analyses of **formal rationality** and **substantive rationality.** The weakening of the religious roots in ascetic Protestantism of the work ethic in capitalist society is one indication of the waning of importance of ultimate values or substantive rationality in modern society. In Weber's view, the absence of these ultimate values in life give it less real meaning.

These views of human nature suggest that individuals and the community are frequently in conflict with each other at the same time that they often need each other. To characterize the tie between the individual and society as a proverbial love/hate relationship would not be far off the mark. The idea that human beings have some essential characteristics independent of their involvement in the community further suggests that people's needs may be frustrated or realized, depending on the organization of society and how they fit into it.

THE INDIVIDUAL AND THE COMMUNITY:
A DELICATE BALANCE

What happens when individuals rub elbows with the community or larger society? As I said earlier, the answer depends on what one thinks people are really like. As a group, the classical theorists had complex and varying views of the relationship between the individual and society. Generally, these images suggested that it contained interdependence and hostile elements, and that the peculiar shape of the relationship depended on various social conditions. For example, although Marx believed that humans were basically social in nature, he certainly felt that the concentration of productive private property in capitalist society made it difficult for individuals such as workers to relate to each other as equals and for people in general to develop to their full potential. In the absence of private property, Marx thought that much of the antagonism, exploitation, and alienation that characterized social relationships would disappear and that individuals and community, as two sides of the same coin, would coexist in harmony with each other. Since individuals are naturally social for Marx, there would be a mutually supportive network developed that would benefit both the individual and society. In the meantime, however, capitalism would continue to limit the development of human potential.

Like Marx, Weber believed that modern individuals were increasingly trapped by forces beyond their control. Large bureaucracies, within which we work, control much of our lives, and the state appears as a remote, inaccessible entity manipulating us from afar. The capitalist form of society is exploitative of the workers who earn their livings working within it. Weber had a tragic view of modern culture, seeing individuals as operating within an "iron cage" of relationships and organizations from which there was little chance of escape. All this suggests a basic hostility between individuals and society. At the same time, however, Weber argued that individuals in Western capitalist societies such as the United States are often filled with a capitalist spirit that encourages the belief that the individual is autonomous and responsible for his or her own fate. Individuals are not victims, but creators of their situations and the society around them. And if their actions are guided by a broad set of values that consider the welfare of others, then the conflict between individuals and society can be minimized.

Simmel's juxtapositioning of *objective* culture as a constraining part of the outside community and *subjective* culture as human creativity suggests that the community and the individual are in conflict.

> The individual strives to be an organic totality, a unity with its own centre from whence all the elements of his being and his action derive a coherent and consistent meaning. But if the supra-individual whole [society] is supposed to be independently coherent and to realize its own objective notion of itself... then it cannot possibly tolerate any independence on the part of its members.... The totality of the whole... stands in eternal conflict with the totality of the individual.[8]

Simmel's view of this relationship was not wholly negative, however. The freedom to be unique is enhanced in large social circles or societies. While it strives toward self-integration, the urban modern society also provides a context in which the individual can freely move and develop to become more unique. Since individuals seek freedom and uniqueness as well as attachment and identification with others, their relationship to society is a fundamentally ambivalent one. It is in the conflict with each other that the identities of both individuals and communities are realized. We find out who we are and what we are made of. One might say, then, that this confrontation has both integrating and disintegrating outcomes.

Durkheim also suggested a mixed view of the relationship between the individual and community, arguing that, on the *social* level, too much egoism weakens the integration of a community and our feelings of obligation to others, and, on the *individual* level, egoism removes much of the social support that individuals need in their everyday lives. Attachment to networks of social relationships with others means that individuals will not have to rely only on their own resources when difficulties arise. On the other hand, too much attachment and community in an individual's life means an overweaning, potentially suffocating regulation of that life. Although the infusion of community culture into the individual is necessary for guidance and solidarity in society, the intrusion into all areas of one's private life can also be threatening. Since contemporary society's features require both autonomy and allegiance, a balance must be reached between individuals' egoistic and social tendencies. Durkheim believed that individuality and social integration/regulation were not incompatible and that modern society could support both. For both Simmel and Durkheim, modern civilized individuals and society exist *through* each other.

Unfortunately, the characterization and understanding of the complexity of the relationship between the individual and society/community in public debates is not often as balanced and thorough as those displayed by classical thinkers. Durkheim, for example, considered *egoistic* individualism, which focuses only on selfish needs, as being profoundly different from a *moral* individualism, which honors "the individual in general" (i.e., has a "sympathy" for all individuals).[9] Egoism as a concern only for self has certainly been ballyhooed as a problem in the contemporary United States. For example, the web page for the Association for California Tort Reform complains that unnecessary lawsuits cost all of us billions of dollars every year because individuals do not want to take responsibility and are interested solely in actions that benefit themselves. One author laments that the United States has become "a nation of finger pointers" who blame everyone but themselves for everything that goes wrong in their lives.[10] Thus, for example, we find people who file a "lawsuit against the dairy industry because someone drank too much milk and the lawsuit against a city by the burglar who was bitten by the police dog during a capture."[11] Claims of individualism gone haywire do not stop here, however. A high level of crime has also been associated with too much individualism.[12] Individualism has even been suggested as a hindrance when it comes to people's attempts to cope with death in their lives. Being cut off from society, individuals in contemporary society feel "uncertain, socially unsupported and vulnerable when it comes to dealing with death."[13]

How have we come to this? Why has individualism taken on such negative tones? Several of the classical theorists believe that the prominence of money in our lives is involved. In his characteristically dialectic style, Simmel, for example, suggested that because money allows so wide an array of potential contacts and relationships, and makes us more dependent on individuals in general, "we are remarkably independent of every *specific* member of . . . society." This helps create a feeling of "inner independence, a feeling of individual self-sufficiency." Even though it ties us together, money "is none the less the breeding ground for economic individualism and egoism."[14] The cash nexus that Marx saw as prevalent in capitalist society encourages us to see others in terms of their use/value to us as commodities. This does not build a feeling of community in individuals.

How are we to address this perceived lack of integration between the individual and community? What are we to do about this apparent pathological individualism? One recent and growing response has been *communitarianism*. Amitai Etzioni, a sociologist and major force in the communitarian movement, says that this philosophy focuses on "the twin need to curb the minting of rights and to balance existing ones with greater willingness to shoulder responsibilities and commitments to the common good. We emphasize the importance of community, the moral claims staked by shared needs and futures, as distinct from the claims of various subgroups and individuals."[15]

Communitarians are attempting to find a middle ground between extreme individualism, which takes no account of the community, and authoritarianism, which takes no account of the individual. With his concept of moral individualism, Durkheim tried to define such a middle ground. Individuals' rights need to be protected, Etzioni argues, but people also need to realize they are part of a larger community to which they are responsible. Durkheim felt that the interdependence demanded in the modern division of labor would make us aware of and sensitive to our obligations to others, and that the social dimension of our selves would grow at the expense of pure egoism. The trick, of course, is in finding and retaining the balance between egoistic and social demands. For Durkheim, the division of labor helps provide this balance. While its specialization fosters individuality, the division of labor is also a moral phenomenon because it takes us out of ourselves and connects us with others.

Sounding very much like Durkheim, Etzioni believes that the family and school, as fundamental institutions in our communities, are where basic moral values need to be taught. But what if these institutions or adherence to a narrow community-based set of values become oppressive? Etzioni replies too facilely that one can always move to a different community.[16] But then how does one integrate all these different communities of values? Can a pluralistic society such as the United States be a stable and cohesive society or does too much pluralism threaten the cohesiveness and integrity of this society? The devil is always in the details.

The controversy about the appropriate relationship between the self and society has reared its head not only in arguments about private rights and public responsibilities but also in a number of other recent debates about growing social concerns. As I will demonstrate next, invasions of privacy through the computer, and rising suicide rates among youth are each issues involving the individual/ society relationship.

THE PUBLIC EYE IN THE PRIVATE LIFE

The computer (more specifically, the World Wide Web) is an increasingly important means by which the community and individuals become linked. Technology has allowed people to develop their unique interests but has also made it possible for outsiders to access the private lives of individuals. In essence, technology can set us free as well as open us to the manipulation of others.

The implementation of a cybernetic information highway has been viewed with both optimism and concern. The World Wide Web has given people the opportunity to find and develop new relationships or to renew old ones. Chatrooms have permitted us to share our problems with others. A virtual community of communication has been created by the transnational spread of computer networks. Computer technology has also made it possible for individuals to work out of their homes, in effect, creating new lifestyles. This is an example of the liberating effects of technology for which Marx hoped.

The rapid and ever-changing advances in technology have also made it possible for almost anyone with access to a computer to tap into databanks containing information on almost any topic imaginable. The World Wide Web allows us to become detectives searching for bits of data on almost anything or anyone in whom we are interested. This facility has greatly extended our ability to probe and thereby enhanced our personal freedom. We have access to information that was never before available, and its amount accelerates by the minute, resulting in an information glut.

It has become increasingly difficult for anyone or anything to escape this ever-widening network of information. "Massive consumer databases are continually sprouting all over the place, some of which are even available free on the

Internet. More important, huge amounts of data about (almost) everyone and everything are available for sale everywhere."[17] We are moving toward a "glass village" in which everyone is available for view online. Moreover, since interconnected technologies have become cheaper for manufacturers to produce, we are developing "a world in which everything is connected to everything else. . . . No matter how deep and well-argued privacy concerns become, however, it is hard to imagine any combination of steps or circumstances that could block the deployment of such technology." Being able to hide and remain anonymous in the complex environs of the metropolis has become more difficult because of the web's power to expose information about all of us.[18] This is both promising and worrisome if we believe, as the classical theorists did, that our human nature has both social and egoistic dimensions or that technology has the potential to either entrap or liberate us. "Technology . . . will allow us to be whatever we are already—only more so."[19] As Simmel advised, the form and content of social phenomena are analytically separate. As a *form,* technology is a powerful instrument. How it is used and what we put into it in the way of *content* is something else entirely. Moreover, technology's usage will be affected by the social, political, and economic context in which it operates.

Technology may be used to bring us together. Some research suggests that relationships created through involvement in chatrooms may be just as meaningful and deep as those created in physical communities. Relationships appear to develop that often expand through other media (phone calls, e-mail, etc.) and into wider sets of relationships.[20] Yet we still know very little about the character, bases, and stability of these relationships compared to those created through face-to-face interaction. Online communication also creates new and perhaps greater opportunities for impression management and duplicity. Anyone who has a message to sell can get a web page and present himself or herself in the most favorable manner. There is almost nothing that has not been said, exposed, debated, and probed in talk media.

At the same time, it is easy to be lulled into the belief that what we do or say online is somehow anonymous, because, like phone conversations between strangers, our faces and real identities are hidden and we are removed from immediate harm. But the anonymity becomes illusory as more conversations occur and technology progresses. Indeed, over time, online communication between individuals becomes more personal, exposing more of a person's private life. A good example of this is the recent case of an individual who confessed to murder over the Internet. Larry Froistad admitted over e-mail to members of his support group that he had killed his daughter. Some members of his support group, as readers of his message, sought to comfort him, apparently too caught up in their online allegiance to realize that an actual murder may have taken place.

Why would anyone publicly confess murder to a number of "strangers" over the Internet? Perhaps one develops a level of comfort with those of similar interest who have taken the time to talk with one another. As some research suggests, under such conditions, more intimacy develops. The feeling of intimacy may be one reason for such a public confession. On the other hand, as one member of Larry's support group put it: "Ultimately, we are alone. The closeness is for the most part illusory. If Larry walked into a room, I wouldn't know him. On line, they're just words on a screen."[21] One analyst suggests that such talk "feels safe.... You're just talking to the screen. Sometimes people get oblivious to the dangers and they say things they wouldn't have said otherwise."[22] The feeling of anonymity, coupled with a sense of comfort about those who are reading the message, may encourage an illusion of invulnerability regarding one's private statements. Ironically, it may be this very sense of safety that allows breaches of one's privacy. What is public is thought to be private, and what is private becomes public. The sense of security and comfort provided by the Internet is perhaps best personified by the woman who recently and willingly gave birth over the Internet.[23]

Chatting and broadcasting over the Internet is not the only growing form of communication between individuals, however. Talk-radio and TV talk shows have become extremely popular as substitutes for the face-to-face relationships that people do not have time to develop in their hectic lives. "It all serves the simple need for connections with other people. People don't know their neighbors anymore, and they wouldn't have time to talk over the backyard fence even if they did. But there's still a human need for community, so it's a virtual, electronic, global media community.... People are looking for a community of like minds."[24] This is a community of talk, however, not physical action, presence, or commitment. As such, there is a real question about the accountability and responsibility within such virtual communities. The confines and limitations created by the geographic fixity and physical presence of others in traditional communities create practical social consequences that pressure people into greater feelings of accountability and responsibility. Even though one's commitment to an online relationship may be just as strong as one created in a more traditional fashion, the perceived character of its consequences may be altered.

As technology allows us to move from communities based on place and physical relationships to one based on "like minds," the relationship between individuals and the community shifts, along with the definition of community. In the Internet, there are as many communities as there are self-interests. In "communities of like minds," individuality and community intersect because individuals with similar unique interests create virtual communities, and such communities are tied together by this interest homogeneity. Durkheim foresaw cohesion in modern society as being based primarily on the union of interests. Each community is a union of minds. In this environment, there is no conflict between these segmented individuals and the community.

In addition to the easy familiarity created in web communities, the proliferation of talk networks in the media also increases the probability that what is private will become public. And what is public and valuable can always be for sale. The self-interest of individuals, the private sale of information, and the desire for private profit all make concerns about invasions of privacy through new technology realistic. Private investigators collect detailed information about individuals without their knowledge and without their even knowing such information about them was available. Information about one's personal finances and assets, medical records, employment history, and telephone records are all accessible to one who knows where to look. In 1992, an explosion at the Texaco plant in Wilmington, California, resulted in personal-injury lawsuits by thousands of individuals. Texaco hired an investigator to probe into the backgrounds of those filing the lawsuits. He did so over a five-year period:

> One claimant, a 23-year-old mother, . . . was frightened to learn that the investigator had generated a five-page computer printout from her name alone. The private eye had found her Social Security number, date of birth, every address where she had ever lived, the names and telephone numbers of past and present neighbors, even the number of bedrooms in a house she had inherited, her welfare history, and the work histories of her children's fathers.

In addition, the investigator found out about two unpaid traffic tickets, which he used as leverage to get information from her about the lawyers representing her case.[25]

Knowing that such information is in demand by those seeking to make or avoid paying out money, dozens of websites representing private companies have sprung up, offering to sell such data to anyone who wants it. Information on one's salary, unlisted phone numbers, and bank account numbers are available for under $100.[26] Of course, data are also available to the average person who is trying to win a battle with someone more powerful or who is trying to get information that will improve the quality of his or her life. A number of privacy bills are pending in Congress, but the invasion and surveillance of individuals' lives through the traffic and transfer in the buying and selling of data across the information highway is only likely to intensify. This is also true of the battles between those who argue for open individual access to such information and those who wish to keep their privacy protected, and between those who seek private gain against the public good. When coupled with the implications of the web for communication between individuals, it is clear that computer technology has significant consequences for individuals and their ties with each other. Such technology can either seduce us into a more private, insular world or expand and open our worlds to others.

Whether use of the Internet creates more isolated or socially involved individuals continues to be an important issue. In one of the most thorough investigations yet, researchers at Carnegie Mellon University followed 169 Internet users for a one- to two-year period. Their careful analysis, involving a large number of controls, found that instead of strengthening social ties and increasing social involvement, Internet usage over time resulted in *decreases* in family communication and maintenance of social relationships and *increases* in loneliness and depression. These findings appear to support the belief that web usage isolates individuals and weakens ties within physical communities.[27]

The expanding use and controversy about the Internet and similar technologies would not have been a great surprise to Durkheim. As societies become more modern, he predicted not only advances in technology but also an intensification of the conflict between the egoistic and social sides of our natures. This conflict has manifested itself in the controversies about the use and abuse of information on the web. In outlining the development of modern society, Durkheim also observed that communities move from those based on kinship and place to those founded on similarities of interests. This technology has lessened the limitations imposed by place and kinship and has accelerated the growth of communities of interest.

The greater use of the Internet is also encouraged by a (perhaps false) sense of security bred by the apparent anonymity of communication among a multitude of strangers. At least initially, this sensation is not unlike the consequences of anonymity experienced in large cities, as discussed by Simmel. Such anonymity allows freedom of expression and individuality. Moreover, as Simmel noted, strangers are often seen as being more objective. Thus, one is willing to tell a stranger intimacies that would not be told to a close friend.

The creation of new markets is another reason for the expansion of the World Wide Web. As Marx, Weber, and Simmel argued, the exchange of money as a universal medium ties individuals together. In the open computer technology, such exchange in the form of data-for-sale creates obligations and dependencies between buyers and sellers. At the same time, it creates another means by which the powerful can manipulate and exploit the less powerful. Within a capitalist economy, in which profit is the central objective, the proliferation of databanks is no surprise. For Marx and Weber, in capitalist societies, economic interests override the power associated with one's status or associational memberships. The economic system of capitalism is "the most fateful force in our modern life."[28] As long as there is an economically based demand and little governmental regulation of access to information about private lives, such databanks will flourish. Marx is most relevant in this scenario. Private interest groups attempt to create and maintain structures and influence policies that serve their purposes. The interests of the community are presented as being less important than or as synonymous with the private objectives of powerful groups. The marketing of ideologies is used to convince constituents and policymakers of this interpretation. Even though the information highway is a two-way street that allows the little person as well as the more powerful open access to information about others, Marx would conclude that it is not a fair fight because of the greater resources of some.

The fact that privacy and its invasion has become such an issue and that little of significance has been done about it suggests that more time has been spent developing and perfecting the technology than worrying about its moral and ethical implications. The latter issues generally lose out to technology in a capitalist, individualistic society. Purely economic interests care nothing for ethics or others; nothing is sacred.

The moral implications of technology and its potential misuse were of deep concern to the classical theorists. For Marx, technology was basically neutral. If privately owned, it can be used to gain personal profit while exploiting others. If not privately owned, it can provide humanity with freedom from the drudgery of onerous tasks and freedom to pursue higher and more fulfilling goals. Weber and Simmel were both concerned with the invasion of objective culture, rationalization, and powerful institutional forces into the lives of individuals because of their potential as instruments of control. They were certainly less sanguine than Marx or Durkheim about the liberating potential of modern technology. Weber was ambivalent about the drive for efficiency and rationality, capitalism's most central characteristic, for while it improves production at less economic cost, it is not sufficient for civilizing a society. It is no substitute for substantive rationality, or the production of a society based on ultimate basic values. Such values should allow us to assess the human worth and consequences of advanced technologies. That something *can* be done technologically or scientifically does not necessarily mean that it *should* be done. Communal human values should override technological development for its own sake or for the sake of a powerful few. Unfortunately, Weber felt that in modern society formal rationality has far outpaced the growth of substantive rationality. In asking whether the technological creation of cyberspace constitutes progress, Weber would ask whether it makes us a more civilized and humane society. This is still an open question, and one that society has spent little time answering.

Like many characteristics of modern society, technology is a double-edged sword. It can free us or enslave us. Technology can be a weapon as well as an enabler. For Marx, everything depends on who controls it. Simmel also would see it as a means by which we can develop our individuality, but also something that can cut us off from others. As adults and children sit in front of their computer screens, hour after hour, their lives become more privatized at the same time that they expose themselves to others by their involvement in information networks. Paradoxically (and Simmel loved paradoxes), computers make us more individualistic and insular, while at the same time they open relationships with others and make our lives more public. They can separate our interests and cause us to withdraw or they can serve as a basis for communion with others. They have both disintegrating and integrating potentials.

SEPARATION AND SUICIDE

The classical theorists viewed humans as fundamentally social in nature. We need others because we develop as human beings in the company of others. On the other hand, argued Durkheim, too much integration into or too much regulation by society is a threat to the individual, as is too little integration or regulation. Too much threatens to engulf and erase the individual, as in a religious cult, whereas too little leaves the individual isolated without support and guidance, as in someone who is cut off from society. In the last section, we saw how the broader community's *intrusion into* individuals' lives can jeopardize their privacy. In this brief section, I will focus on a converse problem—how individuals' *isolation from* the community is related to suicide among youth.

For Durkheim, too much individualism in society can be just as life threatening for the individual as too much community. Durkheim drew a close connection between the level and type of integration in a society and its suicide rate and predominant form.[29] Societies that are homogeneous, generally small, and with strong collective consciousnesses do not permit or encourage the development of the individual as a separate person. Rather, it is group, not individual, identity that is most important. These societies are tightly integrated and highly regulated. They offer clear parameters and guidance for social roles and behavior.

Imagine a small rural community of the past in which people knew each other intimately, in which sameness, religion, and kinship were major sources of solidarity. When individual identities are swallowed up in a society or group, **altruistic suicide,** committed because of one's identity with the group, is the most dominant form of suicide. When individuals have their own identities but perceive few opportunities for themselves or feel overregulated or crushed by the weight of society, **fatalistic suicide** takes precedence as the most likely form. **Anomic suicide** is more prominent when the opposite condition is present—that is, when there is a general absence of any *normative regulation* and guidance of the individual by society. When there is a coherent social structure but individuals are not socially integrated into it, **egoistic suicide** is more likely. Individuals need to be integrated into society to be morally guided by it. When they are not, higher egoistic suicide rates can result because the person does not benefit from the social support of others. In times of stress, they are left to their own devices. It is this form of suicide that Durkheim expected to be most prevalent in individualistic modern society.

Durkheim was undoubtedly concerned on the macrolevel with the integration of society and groups, but he was also concerned on the microlevel with the integration of the individual into society. The two are inextricably bound together:

> Society cannot disintegrate without the individual simultaneously detaching himself from social life.... The more weakened the groups to which he belongs, the less he depends on them, the more he consequently depends only on himself and recognizes no other rules of conduct than what are founded on his private interests. If we agree to call this state egoism, ... we may call egoistic the special type of suicide springing from excessive individualism."[30]

It is estimated that in recent years, about 30,000 Americans have committed suicide every year, and youth suicide, especially among minorities, has been rising. Suicide among youth appears to be significantly related to the "excessive individualism" referred to by Durkheim. Personal isolation and a lack of family integration, social contacts, and support all put adolescents at a higher risk for suicide.[31] On the social level, regions with lower church membership rates and higher percentages of divorced people have higher suicide rates, again suggesting the importance of integration as a protective factor.

Suicide rates seem to be rising especially quickly among African American youth. Between 1980 and 1995, the rate among African American males increased 146 percent, compared to only 22 percent among white males. The gap between the suicide rates of these groups appears to be narrowing. Problems of integration and fatalism have been offered as possible explanations for the rising rate among African American youth. Analysts suggest that the difficulties encountered by the African American middle class in integrating effectively into society, coupled with the accompanying growth of divisions and individualism within the African American community, may be a principal cause of these rate increases. In addition, the growing fatalism of African American youth in the inner city may contribute to a growing hopelessness.[32] West argues that nihilism—a sense of meaninglessness and lovelessness that "breeds a coldhearted, mean-spirited outlook that destroys both the individual and others"—is the primary threat facing today's African American community.[33] A sense of being

COMPARATIVE CHART 3.1   Basic Ideas from Each Theorist Used in Analyses of Chapter Issues

	Individual and Society	Privacy and Technology	Suicide
Marx	Humans basically social, but alienation, exploitation, cash nexus exist in capitalist society due to private property	Technology neutral but private ownership of technology creates potential abuses; data for sale and profit motive of web use; marketing of ideologies and manipulation	Exploitation, economic domination, alienation, market mentality in capitalism linked to taking of human life
Durkheim	Society must be in individual and individual in society; moral individualism and balance of social and egoistic parts of nature needed	Social and egoistic sides of self clash over technology's uses; technology creates integration based on interest instead of kinship or place	Excessive egoism, too little or too much regulation, and too much integration linked to egoistic, anomic, fatalistic, and altruistic types of suicide
Simmel	Rational and nonrational, egoistic and sympathetic sides to human nature; objective vs. subjective culture clash; society and individual each seek integration and identity; individual freedom in large social circles	Form vs. content of technology; anonymity, stranger status, individuality, and freedom encouraged by Internet; web creates closeness and distance	
Weber	Individuals seek meaning through different forms of action; state, bureaucracies, capitalism create remoteness between individual and society; society as iron cage	Computer and web indicators of formal rationality, not necessarily substantive rationality	

trapped encourages the fatalism that promotes suicide. Marx's depiction of a capitalist society—as one in which exploitation, power, and economic dominance play the central roles—makes more understandable the sense of those on the lower rung of society as feeling trapped.[34] Capitalism creates and feeds alienation among and within people. Individualism encourages social isolation, and a market mentality demeans the value of human life.

CONCLUSION

The fact that classical theorists viewed human beings as possessing contradictory natures led them to argue that the relationship between individuals and society would be a complex and often ambivalent one. It is often a confrontational relationship, as well. The primary ideas drawn from theorists to understand each of the issues explored in this chapter are shown in Comparative Chart 3.1.

The controversies over individual rights and public responsibilities, privacy and its invasion by the public, exemplify the ambivalence and complexity of this relationship. At the same time, these theorists recognized that the meaningful attachment of the individual to a community or society is a necessity for healthy lives and social stability. The meaning of one's life is dependent on such engagement. This does not mean that the individual must merge or become one with the society. Rather, the person can prosper as a separate individual and grow as a moral human being only when she or he becomes involved with society. In the next chapter, I will explore two social forms that make such social contact difficult.

QUESTIONS TO PONDER

1. If individuals are both selfish and social, how can a balance in these tendencies best be achieved? Is Durkheim's insistence that the individual must be in society and society in the individual a suitable one?

2. Is private ownership of the Internet more beneficial or harmful to its users? What dangers would Marx foresee? With the expansion of the World Wide Web, should the private and public spheres of life be kept separate? Is computer technology itself neutral?

3. Simmel and Weber both knew that individuals try to maintain their integrity through the creation of distinct identities in society. If this is healthy or necessary, then how could isolation from others be related to suicide or any other pathology?

CHAPTER 4

SEPARATISM AND STATUS

CHAPTER IN BRIEF

- **INTRODUCTION**
issue of social and physical separation;
importance of space as indicator of social
forces

- **THE ARRANGEMENT OF SPACE**
conflict between content and form;
content expressed in form; social features
of space; social distance and social
classifications; increased study of social
space (Simmel)

- **GATED COMMUNITIES**
number, characteristics, and trends;
importance of control and power; three
orders of society (Weber); gated
communities as status groups (Weber);

amorphous nature of gated communities
(Weber); exclusivity and self-containment (Weber); gated communities as
reflections of class; wealthy's manipulation of residential laws; history of Beacon
Hill; class and political power (Marx)

- **RACIAL GHETTOS**
ghettos vs. gated communities; extent of
residential segregation; forces underlying
segregation and its continuation (Marx);
white attitudes about segregation;
segregation, caste, and race (Weber);
legitimation of racism (Weber);
importance of numbers and proportions in
acceptance of segregation (Simmel)

INTRODUCTION

In the last chapter, I emphasized the importance of integrating individuals and
groups into the broader society, suggesting that both individuals and society are
enriched by the open interplay between the two and by the pluralism that results.
Although the umbilical relationship between the individual and society is not
always harmonious, such conflict frequently has positive results for both. Problems of integration are most likely to occur when the interaction among individuals and groups is restricted or limited, or when the social distance between them
is increased. In this chapter, I discuss the issue of social and physical separation

between groups in society and how classical theorists might account for and approach an understanding of these developments. In a general sense, all these theorists believed that as societies progressed, the social relationships and groups that developed in them would be increasingly less constrained by place or geographic boundaries. Relationships would be founded more often on personal and professional interests and would span across space. Nontangible emotional and intellectual forces would become more prominent as the social significance of the physical environment receded.

Nevertheless, where people live and how they live in those areas still tells us about the *social* and *cultural* organization of a society. Specifically, I will focus on gated communities and racial ghettos as spatial arrangements in cities that reflect underlying racial, ethnic, and class processes. The physical patterning and placement of neighborhoods, business centers, and housing developments are a manifestation of underlying beliefs, resource distributions, and prejudices. Where we live and in what we live says something about our social positions in society.

THE ARRANGEMENT OF SPACE

I vividly remember being struck when, on my first plane flight, I looked out the window to see a neat patchwork of carefully bounded, variously colored fields stretching over the countryside. How neat and orderly the landscape appeared from that vantage point. What we seldom realize when we see this pattern is that such arrangements are not arbitrary or fixed, but purposely created for a variety of social and personal reasons. The content of our individual lives—personal dispositions, thinking, and tendencies—becomes socially important only when it brings about a particular structure to a relationship between individuals. The specific *content* of our individual purposes and motives are only realized when they take *form* in interaction with others. A feeling must be manifested in action, just as a creative impulse results in a product. When seen in this light, argued Simmel, content and form are inseparable in reality. "Any social phenomenon or process is composed of two elements which in reality are inseparable: on the one hand, an interest, purpose, or a motive [i.e., content]; on the other, a form or mode of interaction among individuals *through which, or in the shape of which, that content attains social reality.*"[1] At the same time, however, Simmel saw a contradiction between life's processes as represented in content and life's structural manifestations as represented in form. The fixity of form contrasts with the "eternal flux" of life: "life is always in latent opposition to the form."[2] Life is always for growth and change, whereas, like straightjackets, social structures (forms) demand acceptance on their own and obstruct such growth. Life can "express itself and realize its freedom only through forms," but forms, in turn, only "suffocate life and obstruct freedom."[3]

There is no escape from this contradiction and this is part of the tragedy of modern culture. The struggle between these two elements is inevitable and unending. This means that the physical arrangements and forms within a city can be viewed as the physical product of vibrant social, cultural, and psychological processes. At the same time, however, the structures created come to dominate us and restrict our free relations with others. Personal desires and interests (e.g., concerns about security, etc.), shared with others, may cause some to join with others in a relationship that takes the form of a restricted residential community. This form that defines our relationship with others inside and outside the group then becomes a part of objective reality, and the rules and expectations which govern it become a part of objective culture. This entire process pushes society in the direction of greater pluralism and division rather than homogeneity: "The energy inherent in life to create forms that transcend life is a force toward cultural diversity, not unity."[4] As the desire to express individuality intensifies in modern society, the parallel centrifugal process toward more distinctive groups may also accelerate. One manifestation of this distinctiveness lies in the space within which groups live and the location of that space in relation to that of other groups.

The arrangements of objects in space was a special concern to Georg Simmel, and his general comments have particular relevance for our understanding of how and why bounded areas in cities are home to different groups. What is interesting about Simmel's understanding of space is that he addresses its broad social, not physical, dimension. How things (i.e., objects, groups, individuals, institutions) are arranged in space tell us a great deal about social forces at work: "The spatial forms of objects and occurrences are often of great importance, not as causes, but as effects that throw light on the character of the actual forces. The spatial conditions of an occurrence are often very indicative of the processes which have brought it about.... An investigation of the spatial aspect of sociological forms will therefore throw light on the character of the processes of [social interaction]."[5] It is social relationships that define space and create arrangements within it.

Simmel argued that space is defined socially according to several features. First, space is always exclusive and unique, in that particular structures are attached to specific locations. In this case, for instance, one's social identity and place of residence are reciprocally tied together. For example, in his study of enclaves in the United States, Abrahamson observes that "it is the wealthier and more privileged classes who almost always win the competition for the most desirable residential areas. As a result, in many cities there is a marked correlation between the social status of communities and the number of feet at which they rest above sea level."[6]

A second characteristic of space is that it can be broken down into parts, each of which can become a separate area. Like the frame on a picture, each spatial area has boundaries that separate it from others. The boundary suggests the relative self-sufficiency and unity of the group existing in the space. The boundary itself reflects and symbolizes the nature of the social relationship between those inside and outside it: "The border is not a spatial fact with sociological consequences, but a sociological fact that expresses itself in spatial form."[7] Blakely and Snyder begin their study of gated communities by stating simply, "The setting of boundaries is always a political act. Boundaries determine membership: someone must be inside and someone outside . . . . Using physical space to create social place is a long and deep American tradition."[8] As will be discussed, the presence of a gated community with strict security and physical walls tells us something about the perceived relationship between those who live within and those who live outside its boundaries. Boundaries exist in all social relationships and define the point at which access to a person is allowed or prohibited. That boundary may exist at different points, depending in part on the intimacy of the relationship. But there is always a point in a relationship with others beyond which would be violating their privacy. One's "personal space" must be maintained. Boundaries can also be viewed by those within them as being too close or restrictive, or flexible and wide enough to allow for growth of the contained group.

A third important spatial characteristic of social groups is the extent to which the group and its members are tied to a particular "home" or physical location. Such fixity or its absence is a direct manifestation of the strength of a group's unity. Having a particular home or place to which all members can go is a means of maintaining the group's cohesiveness, and conversely of reinforcing its separation from others. Insider/outsider status is made more obvious by the existence of such a home.

Distance and proximity define the fourth social dimension of space. Objects, people, and groups are arranged in social space with given distances and proximities between them. How close or how distant individuals or groups are from each other can affect their social structure. Simmel argued that great distance between the parts of a community make centralization of the community less likely. Control is weakened as the centrifugal force of distance between individuals or groups increases. Distance, of course, can be physical or social in nature. Modern city dwellers may be *socially close* to those in similar professions even though they are *physically distant* from them. In contemporary society, Simmel suggested, group formations are more frequently based on rational or intellectual interests than on kinship or emotional grounds. "The general trend ... often bears a rational character, and ... the substantive purpose of these groups is the result of conscious reflection and intelligent planning."[9] People join with those of similar interests for pragmatic reasons.

On the other hand, urbanites tend to be *socially distant* from those with whom they share few interests, even though they are *physically close* to them. This is indicated by the apparent blasé attitude that characterizes the latter relationships. Groups may care little for each other, or even be unaware of each other's existence, even though they are physically close. I am reminded here of Floyd Hunter's classic study of Atlanta's power structure, in which he observed the fact that by using the expressway on their way home, middle-class professionals could entirely bypass and never see lower-class neighborhoods. Out of sight, out of mind.[10]

In the large city, the social distance between individuals is supported by its size and the usage of various kinds of classifications into which we put people. Most relationships are not between individuals as individuals, but between persons as functions or categories. In the classroom, the relationship is not between John and Mary, but between teacher and student. This makes the relationship less intimate, and therefore less unique. Our knowledge of each other is based only on bits and pieces of information each has of the other. Most of our social relationships are mediated by many such elements from objective culture, causing alienation or a lack of close relationship among individuals. For example, social and cultural stereotypes, work functions, and social positions are often used to interpret and form the basis of social relationships between persons. Rationality, objectivity, functional specialization, and money all mitigate against intimate relationships. They come between people and interfere with the possibility of close, personal relationships. As social forms, the urban spatial arrangements discussed in the next sections define our relationships with others and reflect the interests of given individuals, but as rigid forms they also hinder the full realization of life for many. As Simmel might say, they both reflect and undermine our interests.

As important as spatial arrangements are, however, they have not been a centerpiece in social theory. "The absence of serious reflection on humanity's built environment has been called 'one of the main silences in social theory.'"[11] However, in the last decade, a rising number of scholars have resurrected a focus on the use of space to reflect cultural, economic, political, and social processes. The locations and sizes of offices in a corporation and the location of entrances and exits to buildings for different kinds of people, for example, are symbolic of differences in economic, social, and political power. The association of particular urban spaces and regions with certain subcultures or groups of people also reflect variations in social status. Gated communities of the privileged, ethnic enclaves, and racial ghettos are primary examples of distinct, concentrated, enclosed social formations within the urban setting. Each of these tends to vary in the groups that predominate in them, in their voluntariness, and in their relationships with outsiders.[12] I will focus my application of classical theorists on an understanding of the extremes in this case: gated communities and racial ghettos.

GATED COMMUNITIES

Gated communities have been springing up at a rapid rate in the United States, taking up more and more of the metropolitan landscape. In 1997, it was estimated that there were about 20,000 such communities, most of them appearing since the mid-1970s, and containing over 3 million separate residences.[13] These developments have been variously referred to as *enclaves, citadels,* and *fortresses,* each of which strongly suggests that they are intentionally closed off from the outside. Generally, "gated communities are residential areas with restricted access in which normally public spaces are privatized. They are security developments with designated perimeters, usually walls or fences, and controlled entrances that are intended to prevent penetration by nonresidents."[14] There is protection of insiders through the exclusion of outsiders. It is not unusual for armed guards, stationed at entrances, to check identification for those who wish to enter. If a person is not a resident, chances are slim to none that he or she will be allowed entrance.

Control and order are evident in other ways, as well, from restrictions on street parking, to planned recreational activities, to professional landscaping that restricts the types of plants that can be grown. Residents pay a regular fee for these services, and homeowner associations monitor residential behavior and enforce restrictions on home and property features. They are, in effect, similar to a private government. As an enclave, a gated community "involves a special relationship between a distinctive group of people and a place," a status and lifestyle that is tied to a particular space in the city.[15] Large sections of land in desirable areas all over the country have been bought up by developers hoping to attract home buyers and make a handsome profit. One consequence is that such developments reduce access of less wealthy nonresidents to previously available recreational areas, such as those along the coast. In South Carolina, for example, such communities have "increased racial tension, displaced poorer residents, and polarized communities." In restricting access to the coast, critics complain that "now the ocean is being sold as an amenity."[16] "Gated communities are part of the trend toward exercising physical and social means of territorial control."[17]

But then the "monopolization of ideal and material goods or opportunities" is typical of status groups.[18]

The heavy element of control involved in gated communities as social phenomena suggests the importance of power in the battle over the use of physical space. Those who have power can separate themselves from others and maintain their cultural and social homogeneity by shaping the built environment. Those who seek to live in such communities do so because they seek a safer, more secure environment and/or want to be surrounded by those with similar lifestyles, values, or class position. The motivation, most generally, is to find and be surrounded by a sense of community, to create a security blanket that is pleasant, comforting, and protective.

As gated communities create the illusion of protection, they further isolate individuals and groups from each other. Pockets or "pods" are created in which similar individuals live together separated from those who are alien. In a broad but not necessarily intimate sense, they create cohesion within the group, yet these pockets exacerbate separations between groups and deepen social and cultural fragmentation in society: "Such a development might help some Americans regain the sense of community and safety which many feel they have lost. Yet if America is to parcel itself up into private, patrolled, communities, it is worth remembering that the walled cities of medieval Italy were both a symptom, and a cause, of a society plagued by war."[19] "Gated communities are a symbol of the underlying tensions in the social fabric," write Blakely and Snyder in the conclusion of their study on such communities. "When combined with patterns of racial and economic segregation, income polarization, and exclusionary land use practices, the symbolic impact of gated communities is even more acute."[20] The use of space for gated communities illustrates Simmel's principles regarding the arrangement of space as a sociological phenomenon, and the significance of boundaries, exclusivity, and social distance as features of that space.

Although they can be found in a wide variety of locations within a city, normally gated communities are associated with middle- and upper-class groups. In addition to being a reflection of economic and power inequality, they also bring status distinctions in our society into the foreground. Gated communities represent an effective illustration of Weber's concept of social status and **status groups.** He believed that inequality in society was a reflection of the distribution of power and that it could be based on a variety of grounds. Every modern society has three "orders" that correspond to different types of inequality: social, economic, and political. The **social order** contains status groups that are distinguished by their lifestyles or patterns of consumption and are ranked on the basis of the prestige or "honor" given to them by others. The **economic order** includes hierarchically arranged classes differentiated by their amounts of property and market situation. Finally, the **political order** consists of parties or associations organized to gain power for their members. Some groups obviously have more power than others. Although analytically distinct, each of these three aspects of inequality are interrelated and can be based on each other. In contemporary capitalist society, however, Weber felt that class was the most fundamental of the three types of inequality, and it is most likely that status prestige will be based on class position rather than the other way around. Weber agreed with Marx that social class was the fundamental dimension of inequality in modern society.

Gated communities exhibit status, class, and party-related features. As status groups, gated communities bring together individuals who wish to live a particular lifestyle in terms of common outlook, interests, recreations, and social practices. Their lifestyle is manifested in patterns of consumption—the goods and services that they purchase. The kinds of cars, landscaping, education, hobbies, and social activities in which residents of gated communities engage are displays of their lifestyles. Because of their position and lifestyle, wealthy retirees in retirement communities or young, upcoming professionals in their own walled enclaves are accorded certain amounts of prestige by the wider society. Weber observed that status groups tend to intentionally consume certain kinds of goods and services and avoid others, carry on traditions that are relatively exclusive to their members, and engage in restricted interaction. With respect to the latter, there are usually unwritten rules about the kinds of people with whom one should associate and socialize, and the conditions under which such interaction should or should not occur. In the most extreme cases, there may even be rules and traditions about the groups into which one can marry. These characteristics are found in groups of varying status in society.

Status groups, gangs, construction workers, professors, entrepreneurs, and corporate executives all observe rules and practices of the kinds just indicated. Each contain mechanisms of enforcement for their members and ways of distinguishing insiders and excluding outsiders. Status groups perpetuate themselves as the "bearers of all 'conventions' ... all 'stylization' of life either originates in status groups or is at least conserved by them."[21] As Weber argued, the properties of a common lifestyle and rules regarding associations with others mean that "status groups are normally communities. *They are, however, often of an amorphous kind.*"[22] The latter statement is important for an understanding of gated communities because even though they bring together people who have a common lifestyle or position, and in this sense are a "community," they do not necessarily create a personal intimacy among their residents, and in this sense, they are *not necessarily* a community.

Studies suggest that even though prospective residents of gated communities may expect to find a deep feeling of community with their neighbors, it is not always realized. Neighbors may on occasion socialize and feel comfortable with each other, but they do not usually feel a strong sense of commitment and responsibility for each other. And in those enclaves with upper-class residents who are busy with their traveling or work, there is frequently little time for the development of this mutuality. In fact, the very security that attracted them to a gated community in the first place may keep them from developing lasting relationships within the walls of their community.[23] The "amorphous" nature of the community means that it is based on similarity of lifestyle, interests, or wealth among *types* of people rather than on something more personal among *individuals*. The paradox indicated by this situation suggests again the underlying tension between individuals and community that was addressed in the last chapter.

The move toward self-containment on the part of status groups is primarily carried out to avoid contamination from outsiders. For the purity and expected social environment to be maintained in a gated community, order, predictability, and sameness must be protected. Although the gated communities being discussed were not as prolific in the United States when he was writing, Weber had visited the United States and was well aware that residential location could be a basis for status, in part because of the freedom afforded one in a democracy to choose one's associates: "For example, only the resident of a certain street ('the street') is considered as belonging to 'society,' is qualified for social intercourse, and is visited and invited."[24]

Social distancing and exclusion are the principal devices used by those with power and wealth to protect their lifestyles and control social interaction. Men try to keep women out of coveted occupational positions, and dominant ethnic/racial groups try to keep others out of their territories through the use of their political power and resources. Segregation results. Those with income and wealth use their economic resources as a basis for power and protection of their lifestyles within their exclusionary gated communities. "Status groups are often created by property classes."[25]

In the contemporary United States, status is more often than not tightly bound to wealth. Gated communities of prestige are, of course, not the only means by which the wealthy and powerful have attempted to maintain their positions and lifestyles. Those at the top of the class hierarchy have always tried to isolate themselves from groups below them and have used a variety of mechanisms to maintain their exclusivity. In the extreme case, such separations have been supported by legislation and taken on a castelike character that prevents intermingling between higher- and lower-status groups. Private preparatory schools were devised as a way to perpetuate the social isolation and specialness of the upper class intergenerationally. Such exclusive institutions with economic and other restrictions help to instill the skills, values, breeding, and taste in those who are expected to be advocates for their class.[26] These schools also lay the groundwork necessary for admission into elite universities and ultimately into positions of power in society. In elite prep schools, we see the careful interweaving of status, wealth, and power.

Residentially, exclusion of racial, ethnic, and economic undesirables by the economically powerful has also been practiced historically through the manipulation of zoning rules and restrictive land covenants.[27] The flexibility of zoning rules makes them amenable to the wishes of those with money and influence. Pleas and arguments for zoning changes are most likely to be effective when made by the middle and upper classes. Requirements in an area for large lots, single-family homes, and minimum square footage help ensure that those who will build in the area will be from the same or a similar social class. Restrictive land covenants contain rules that must be observed by anyone building or living in a given area. Like zoning rules, these covenants allow the upper class to control who comes into an area and the kind of lifestyle they can fully practice. A covenant may cover, for example, what kinds of building can and cannot be constructed, as well as their size and location. They can even cover what kind of materials and colors will be permitted in construction.

Another kind of restrictive covenant has historically limited the access of certain ethnic and racial groups to property in a given area. In some cases, a condition of the sale of property was that it would not be sold later to individuals from "undesirable" groups. As late as the early 1960s, for example, it was found that exclusionary procedures were being practiced in the upper-class Grosse Pointe suburbs outside Detroit. A privately hired detective looked into the ethnic/racial backgrounds, occupations, appearances, and lifestyles of prospective buyers, and then reported his results to the Grosse Pointe Property Owners' Association. Different racial/ethnic groups were ranked in a point system according to their desirability. This served as an effective means of screening potential residents by those who worked to keep their enclave free from contamination of outside groups.[28]

Marx was one of the first to explain that the propertied class is also the most powerful group in society, and to suggest how they can use their economic power as a basis for political power. Those who are in formal positions of power are most often from the more privileged classes, and they can shape legislation to favor their own private material interests. The land regulations referred to earlier are a good example of such legislation. Zoning changes to favor well-connected developers are another illustration. The organization of upper-class persons into parties to protect and promote legislation that ensure maintenance of their lifestyles and property is a likely possibility also outlined by Weber, since party can be based on class as well as status position.

Mark Abrahamson describes how a group of wealthy Bostonians were able to manipulate political forces to create Beacon Hill as an upper-class enclave and make sure that Boston Common park was used in a manner that was consistent with the traditional upper-class lifestyle.[29] Late in the eighteenth century, a group of Boston's elite purchased land on Beacon Hill with the purpose of building private residences that would reflect their preferred way of living. Their political connections allowed them to get building permits without delay, to have priority in the publicly funded construction of roads in the area, and to manipulate zoning rules for the protection of the upper-class residential character of Beacon Hill. Next to Beacon Hill is a large park known as Boston Common, which became a subject of class controversy. As befitting their lifestyle, the upper class wanted to maintain the park as a quiet, secure, and pleasant place in which to stroll and admire the natural beauty of carefully constructed lawns and gardens. Working-class Bostonians, on the other hand, were looking for places for recreation not afforded by their neighborhoods, and wished to use the park for picnics and as playgrounds for their children.

The lifestyles of these two groups obviously clashed. "The elite considered working-class people to be dirty and unkempt people who had messy picnics in the parks, drunks who were using the park to 'sleep it off,' immoral adolescents who were seeking sexual orgies in dark parks at night, or roughnecks who were trampling the grass with their ball games."[30] Park authorities sided with the more powerful, upper-class residents and worked to maintain the quality and sacred separateness of upper-class parks while providing working-class residents with poor substitutes that were not much more than "open dumps."[31] Later, the upper class gave their stamp of approval to a public park system, but only after having been convinced that parks' recreation programs could be used to instill obedience and a work ethic in youth, which would serve them well when they became employees of companies owned by the upper class.

The process just described demonstrates how economic power can be translated into political power, and how the power of property ownership can be used to exploit natural resources and other groups. For Marx, of course, this would not be at all surprising. Social classes are always defined in relation to one other, with the position of each depending on the position of the others. For him, the relationship between the upper and working classes was characterized by exploitation. With the use of their ownership and power, the capitalist class exploits the working class by limiting their opportunities (as in the park situation just discussed), controlling their working conditions, and providing only meager wages to their factory-level employees.

The Beacon Hill example also shows, in Marx's terms, how the upper class can move from a **class-in-itself,** consisting merely of individuals and families in similar economic situations, to a **class-for-itself,** consisting of an organized political group marshalling its resources to fight actively for its interests. The intensification of conflict between the classes gives rise to a consciousness of one's membership and stake in a class position on both sides of the conflict. In the process of protecting their interests, the upper class develops and spreads ideologies that justify their actions and support their positions against those of others. Their argument about the "proper" use of parks exemplifies this point. Their economic and political power make it likely that it will be their version rather than that promoted by a lower class that will be accepted as the official and preferred one by public officials who, more likely than not, represent the interests of the upper class.

To paraphrase Marx, the ruling ideas are always those of the rulers, or, as an aberration of the Golden Rule states, He who has the gold rules. It is a group's position in the material world, however, that is fundamental to their rule: "It is always the direct relation between the masters of the conditions of production and the direct producers which reveals the innermost secret, the hidden foundation of the entire social edifice and therefore also of the political form of the relationship between sovereignty and dependence, in short, of the particular form of the State."[32]

Marx believed that human beings were naturally social, but that the capitalist form of society hinders their full social and human development. It does this in large part because of the alienation between groups that it creates. Private ownership of property separates individuals and groups from each other and allows the exploitation of one group by another. As privately owned enclaves, gated communities of the privileged intentionally segregate the upper-class from lower-class groups. Although they may aid in raising the consciousness of the upper class of the similarities and uniqueness of their own group, gated communities also serve to alienate social classes from each other. Marx argued that the character of individuals is directly shaped by what they do and what they create. "As individuals express their life, so they are."[33] If what we create are isolated, exclusive communities, then we will become more isolating and alienating in our characters.

RACIAL GHETTOS

The voluntary segregation associated with privileged gated communities has accelerated throughout the United States. Unfortunately, racial segregation in ghettos, which is much less voluntary, is also a common and intractable feature of the urban landscape. While they display several of the spatial principles of concern to Simmel, such as social distance and boundaries, ghettos represent the opposite end of the status-hierarchy ranking areas in which different kinds of groups are spatially enclosed. In contrast to those who populate gated communities, residents of racial ghettos are generally there involuntarily, feel less secure in their neighborhood, are not accorded high degrees of social honor, have a less fulfilling lifestyle, and are among the poorest in the country. Yet, despite these problems, racial ghettos and segregation have continued virtually unabated, even without the physical walls that characterize gated communities.

Historically, the emphasis in gated communities has been for residents to keep outsiders out, whereas the thrust for ghettos has been for white outsiders to keep blacks in them. "Wide-scale residential segregation has been a continuous fact of urban life since blacks began to move to cities in large numbers in the early twentieth century . . . black ghettos did not progressively break up with each succeeding generation."[34] In their landmark study of racial residential segregation in the United States, Massey and Denton provide hard evidence for the continued and sometimes intensified presence of racial ghettos.[35] Focusing on the 30 metropolitan areas with the largest African American populations, they found that generally there has been no decline in racial isolation or segregation. Two-thirds of blacks live in all-black neighborhoods, and three-fourths of blacks would have to be moved to create integrated neighborhoods or to have the neighborhoods approximate the total distribution of blacks and whites in the metropolitan area. Even when African Americans have moved to the suburbs, most continue to live and be concentrated in areas of poor quality.

In a manner reminiscent of Simmel's approach to understanding the properties of physical space and how spatial arrangements reflect deeper social, economic, and cultural processes, Massey and Denton identify five dimensions of the "spatial arrangement" of African American residential areas: (1) unevenness, (2) isolation, (3) clustering, (4) concentration, and (5) centralization. When all of these are present to a high degree, there is a condition of extreme segregation, or hypersegregation. *Unevenness* refers to the extent to which African Americans are distributed unevenly throughout the metropolitan area. Black neighborhoods may or may not be *concentrated* in given areas. They may also be *clustered* together or spread around the city, or be *centralized* near the center of the city or located near its fringes. Finally, black neighborhoods may contain virtually no whites, giving them little daily opportunity to interact with them, thereby creating a situation of racial "isolation." Massey and Denton found that 16 of the metropolitan areas were hypersegregated. These areas contained over one-third of the African American population in the United States: "People growing up in such an environment have little direct experience with the culture, norms, and behaviors of the rest of American society and few social contacts with members [of] other racial groups. Ironically, within a large, diverse, and highly mobile post-industrial society such as the United States, blacks living in the heart of the ghetto are among the most isolated people on earth."[36]

Many African Americans live in what have been called "outcast ghettos," made up largely of the poor who, by and large, have been left out of the mainstream economy.[37] These are areas in which there is not only a concentration of African Americans but also a concentration of poor people. They are areas in which the informal economy is dominant and in which local businesses serve only local residents. Socially and economically, the people in these areas are isolated from the rest of society. Although the outcast ghetto's residents are citizens and are still subject to the laws of society, their power in national political processes is minimal.

The isolation and poverty of the ghetto appears to be propelled by a combination of forces, including racial segregation in housing, shifts in the nature and distribution of jobs within the occupational structure, weakness of educational institutions, and the exodus of middle-class African Americans from the central city. Studies have shown that residential segregation and the difficulties encountered by African Americans in moving to better homes and neighborhoods have been abetted by governmental policies. The Federal Housing Authority (FHA), founded in the mid-1930s to help spark the economy, practiced *redlining*, in which maps of neighborhoods that were considered too risky for loans were colored red, and more often than not, these were central-city neighborhoods in which minorities predominated. This meant that the FHA was much more willing to award loans to those building single-family suburban homes than they were to supporting home construction or improvement in the central city. Members of the agency also worked with the assumption that the separation of blacks' and whites' homes through racial segregation would maintain the stability of housing values.[38] A more recent study by the Federal Reserve found that blacks were two to three times as likely as whites to be denied bank loans for home purchases. In some cities, blacks were turned down even though their incomes were significantly higher than those of whites who were approved for loans.[39]

In sum, broad economic shifts, governmental policies, and discrimination have conspired to create more geographic polarization along economic and racial lines. Goldsmith and Blakely summarize these trends in *Separate Societies:* "In essence, jobs are moving to the white nonunion periphery, leaving minority, less-educated city dwellers behind.... The restructuring of metropolitan residential areas whitened the already white suburbs and further concentrated African Americans and Latinos in darker-skinned, central-city areas; wealth and income went to the suburbs and poverty was crowded in the city."[40] As might be suggested by these remarks, racial segregation and poverty concentrations are related. Metropolitan areas that are highly segregated also display significant separations between rich and poor areas.[41] Poverty concentration has also increased in urban areas, especially for African Americans and Puerto Ricans.[42] In this sense, class and race are both factors in the ghetto.

Both Marx and Weber observed that capitalism produces difficulties for those on the lower rungs of the socioeconomic ladder. Both realized that capitalists benefit from the system more than workers. Marx especially understood that those with wealth and power will use a variety of means to maintain and augment their positions. Although he did not pay particular attention to race as a principal variable in accounting for exploitation and dominance, his broad framework has been used to develop class analyses of racial discrimination and models of the racial ghetto as an internal colony dominated by powerful white institutions outside the ghetto.

Marx's general ideas can also be easily adapted to aid in understanding the *perpetuation* of residential segregation. Documented over decades, white racial prejudice showing a lack of firm support for residential integration, and systematic discrimination on the part of governmental, financial, and real-estate institutions appear to be more important than class dynamics in accounting for the *creation* of black ghettos.[43] Class and economic factors become more salient when addressing the *continuation* of ghettos. Marx believed that, for capitalists, the enhancement of profit was always a primary motive for investments. Thus, real-estate agents and bank officers are not likely to stop discrimination in the housing market if they believe that investing in better homes for African Americans or promoting housing integration is not likely to give them a good return on their money. It does not matter whether the ultimate reason for that lack of return is racial prejudice or anything else. The economic motive guides their actions even though it may be informed by racial prejudice. This system helps maintain residential segregation.

Earlier, it was noted that those in federal governmental positions of importance tend to be from the higher social classes. They also tend to be white. Only 1 percent of elected federal positions are occupied by blacks. Considering that those who design policies are largely not only well-to-do but also white, and that, as Marx suggests, they will make policies that serve their own interests, it is not surprising that official legislation and programs have perpetuated gated communities and racial residential segregation as forms of spatial isolation. As mentioned earlier, the broader economic changes brought on by capitalists' drive to compete successfully have also exacerbated residential segregation. The movement of good jobs out of the central city, the proliferation of white-collar office jobs in the suburbs, and the transfer of jobs to other regions and countries are all rationally driven by a profit motive. Finally, although racial prejudice may be more significant in accounting for the creation of ghettos, historically capitalists have used such prejudice as a means of dividing the working class. The possible threat to capitalism of a united working class is minimized if racial ideologies can be used to divide its members. African Americans have been used effectively as strikebreakers and as a surplus army willing to work for lower wages in poor jobs. Fomenting racial prejudice within the white working class works, at least in the short run, to the benefit of capitalists, even though in the long run, such a "taste" for prejudice will damage the chances of taking full advantage of the productivity of labor.

The preference of whites in general to choose neighborhoods that are largely composed of members of their own race can be viewed as an attempt to maintain their own social status. Indeed, surveys find that although most whites believe in integration, in principle, and that people ought to be able to live where they want, in practice most do not want to live in neighborhoods that are at least 50 percent black and most believe that blacks bring down the value of surrounding properties, do not take as good care of their homes as whites, and are more prone to crime and violence than whites.[44] "Given that a home is widely viewed as a symbol of a person's worth, these views imply that whites perceive blacks to be a direct threat to their social status."[45] The kinds of stereotypes that whites possess reinforce the belief that African Americans will damage their lifestyle. Given this belief, it is not surprising that whites would prefer to live in neighborhoods that are predominantly white in racial composition.

The belief on the part of most whites that blacks are qualitatively different (i.e., have different values and lifestyles), and that these opinions appear to be intractable, strongly suggests that many whites believe blacks are basically a different kind of people. Weber argued that the push toward formal exclusion of a group is most likely when the underlying difference between the groups is perceived as being "ethnic" or fixed in nature. He described such relationships as being castelike and as an extreme form of status inequality. As indicated by studies on prejudice and institutional policies that promote residential segregation, "status distinctions are then guaranteed . . . by conventions and laws. . . . The 'caste' is, indeed, the normal form in which ethnic communities usually live side by side in a 'societalized' manner."[46] Relations between African Americans and whites have often been portrayed as a caste system.[47] Certainly, some of these features accurately describe such relations; for example, racial intermarriage and social mobility have been difficult for blacks in the United States.

According to Weber, the forming of status groups on a racial basis is unusual in modern society. Rather, more often than not, status groups are based on class position, because the chances of practicing a particular style of life is heavily dependent on one's economic resources. Nevertheless, under certain conditions, race can be a basis for exclusive status groups. This is especially likely when "objective 'racial differences' are . . . basic to every subjective sentiment of an ethnic community."[48] In the individual case of the United States, Weber apparently worried about the problems raised by the the low status of blacks and the conflict between blacks and whites. During his brief U.S. visit, he did speak with W. E. B. DuBois,[49] who referred to racial prejudice "the problem of the twentieth century."[50] "Only the Negro question and the terrible immigration form a big, black cloud," wrote Weber on his views about the United States "What shall become of these people [African Americans] seems absolutely hopeless."[51] Judging from the fact that residential segregation has not significantly improved despite antiracial legislation, Weber's views about the significance of the racial problem and its likely outcome may not be far off.

Racist ideologies have frequently been used to justify residential segregation and racial inequality in general. Weber was aware that the character of a relationship must be seen as legitimate for it to become accepted by the parties involved and be maintained over time. The legitimation of relationships is a primary means for keeping a social structure of dominance intact. The legitimation of a relationship between a subordinate and superordinate, in Weber's opinion, can be based on the latter's charisma or position, or on tradition. It seems clear that both tradition and formal position have been used in attempts to legitimate the unequal relationships between African Americans and whites. The slavery heritage and stereotypes arising from it, along with scientific racism alleging black inferiority have helped justify discrimination and convince African Americans that their treatment is just. However, these attempts at the latter have generally not been effective.

Despite the lack of support for racist ideologies among African Americans, whites have been able to maintain power over them. "In general, we understand by 'power' the chance of a man or of a number of men to realize their own will in a communal action even against the resistance of others who are participating in the action."[52] In each case, whites have been in the dominant position, and consequently have been able to maintain residential segregation.

White prejudice and discrimination is especially likely to be enacted in a community when the numbers and/or proportion of African Americans reach a particular point. The studies of attitudes toward residential integration cited earlier uncovered a threshold beyond which whites would be unwilling to tolerate integration. Whites are willing to tolerate a small number of blacks in a neighborhood, but would be averse to living in a neighborhood that was one-third black:

> When the number of blacks is small, an open housing market yields neighborhood racial compositions that are within the limits of white tolerance. . . . In a city with a

large black population, however, an open market generates neighborhood racial compositions that are unacceptable to the vast majority of whites. . . . As the proportion of blacks in an urban area rises, therefore, progressively higher levels of racial segregation must be imposed in order to keep the probability of white-black contact within levels that are tolerable to whites.[53]

Simmel could not have said it any better. Having begun with Simmel, it is fitting that we end with him. In his attempt to create a sociology that was essentially a geometry of the social world, Simmel was fascinated with the effect of numbers and proportions on social phenomena and individual behavior. Numbers make a difference and can create a critical mass at which point new phenomena appear. Small groups have qualitatively different characteristics from large ones, and members within each are governed differently. Small changes in numbers can have significant effects on the social structure and relationships within a group. For example, relationships in small groups are more intense and personal than in large groups. Proportions are also important. The impact of a group increases as both the absolute size and the relative proportion of a group increases relative to the society. This would appear to be borne out by those who find that conflicts between African Americans and whites accelerate as the number and proportion of blacks in a neighborhood also increase. We should expect the conflict between whites and minorities to intensify as the proportion of the U.S. population that is minority also increases. Within minority groups, however, we should also expect increasing divisions and disagreements as their size grows. Among African Americans, we already see internal divisions along ideological and economic lines, divisions that have created disunity within their ranks. Simmel saw the division of labor as a source of unity within large groups. In the black community's relationship with whites, it is also a source of disunity.

CONCLUSION

In conclusion, it seems evident that an understanding of the geographic separation and isolation of economic and racial groups can be deepened by using the seminal ideas of the classical theorists, especially Simmel, Marx, and Weber. The relevant ideas and concepts drawn from their work for this analysis are noted in Comparative Chart 4.1. The ideas presented here could have just as easily been applied to the separation and isolation of other groups, such as religious cults, political groups, and lifestyle clusters. Spatial formations and arrangements as manifestations of a society's social structure are always the result of underlying social, political, economic, and numeric forces. Classical theories are detailed attempts to reveal those forces. It is because of their intricate nature and broad

COMPARATIVE CHART 4.1 Basic Ideas from Each Theorist Used in Analyses of Chapter Issues

	Arrangement of Space	Gated Communities	Racial Ghettos
Marx		Role of class and upper-class use of political power to maintain exclusivity; from class-in-itself to class-for-itself	Class interests and class power used to create and maintain segregation
Simmel	Separation of content and form; forms as reflections of social forces; spaces as socially defined, with boundaries, identities, and patterns of social distance and proximity		Numbers and proportions of blacks and whites affect attitudes about racial segregation
Weber		Social, economic, and political orders in society; communities as status groups stressing unique life-style and exclusivity	Racial groups as status groups and castes; use of formal position and tradition to legitimate racial ideologies

scope that these theories are effective in helping to understand current social phenomena.

The previous chapter focused broadly on the integration and separation of the individual and society. This current chapter continued the theme of separation and unity in an examination of two examples of spatial arrangements in the city. Gated communities and racial ghettos are just two manifestations of social distance in U.S. society, however. Social distance between individuals can also be found in the cynicism and distrust within personal relationships and between individuals and government. These are the subjects of Chapter 5.

QUESTIONS TO PONDER

1. Think about how space is arranged around you (i.e., where things are placed, who has access to what areas, etc.). How do these arrangements reflect Simmel's principles of space, especially the idea that spatial arrangements are sociological facts?

2. Gated communities reflect both social pluralism and desires for individuality. What are their consequences for social unity in a free society?

3. Gated communities and racial ghettos are examples of how status groups are residentially separated from each other. What other kinds of status groups also stress spatial exclusivity?

■ ■ ■ ■ ■

CHAPTER 5

THE DECLINE OF CIVILITY
CYNICISM, CORRUPTION, AND OTHER NASTINESS

CHAPTER IN BRIEF

■ **INTRODUCTION**
feelings of cynicism, doubt, and distrust;
core elements of a civil society

■ **SYMPTOMS OF AN UNCIVIL
SOCIETY**
surveys showing lack of personal morals
and trust in institutions; savings and loan
scandal; disillusionment with government; positive fallout from sources of
uncertainty and confusion

■ **UNRAVELING THE ROOTS OF
POLITICAL CORRUPTION**
human nature and corruption (Durkheim);
deviance and social structure (Durkheim);
The Role of Education (Durkheim): moral
behavior as disciplined, impersonal, and
autonomous; need for secular morality;
need for early education and teachers as
role models; means of creating moral
behavior in school; education and reduction of political corruption; *Bureaucracy,
Capitalism, and Corruption* (Weber and

Marx): rational action and bureaucracy;
bureaucracy as impersonal, efficient, and
vulnerable to corruption; bureaucracy as
inhibitor of unethical personal behavior;
bureaucratic vs. patrimonial and charismatic organizations; bureaucracy's affinity with capitalism

■ **THE MISANTHROPIC TENDENCY**
Money Talks (Simmel): positive and negative dimensions of money; elimination of
qualitative and value differences by
money; money as cause of cynicism; *The
Push for Profit* (Marx): capitalism's
stages and drive for profit; recent economic shifts linked to worker distrust;
corporate ideology, belief in individualism, and growth of cynicism; *"Well Whatever":* capitalist spirit and proper use of
wealth (Weber); anomie as root of confusion, injustice, and distrust (Durkheim);
lack of collective assemblies and weak
collective conscience (Durkheim)

INTRODUCTION

In *The Verdict,* a riveting film about legal power and corruption, lawyer Frank Galvin tries to win a case of medical malpractice against formidable odds. The task is so daunting because Galvin is a lone, unknown lawyer with a checkered personal and professional history trying to protect a patient who is a nobody. He is up against an army of lawyers from a famous law firm representing two internationally renowned physicians who carried out an ill-fated operation in a well-known Boston hospital, which has additional legal representation. It is a classic study of a powerless underdog fighting a steep uphill battle. In his summation at the end of the trial, feeling frustrated and desperate, Galvin laments:

> You know, so much of the time we're just lost. Say please God, tell us what is right, tell us what is true. When there is no justice, the rich win; the poor are powerless. We become tired of hearing people lie. And after a time we become dead. We think of ourselves as victims. And we become victims. We become weak. We doubt ourselves. We doubt our beliefs. We doubt our institutions. And we doubt the law.

Frank Galvin obviously feels that there is a lot of confusion about right and wrong and that relationships among us are not what they should be (i.e., full of trust, compassion, consideration, and honesty). He believes the daily bombardment of corruption results in our turning away from others and society in general. We become cynical and distrusting; we turn inward and become ineffectual citizens.

In a word, the United States becomes less of a "civil society." The core aspects of a civil society appear to involve structural and evaluative dimensions. On the *structural* side, a civil society consists of all those social relationships and associations in which individuals are involved. This aspect addresses our connectedness with each other, our sociability. The *evaluative* dimension of a civil society refers to the "quality of our social life, including safety, mortality, civility, respect for diversity, and social order" as well as "civil liberties" and "social justice."[1]

This characterization comes close to what Durkheim meant by *civilization.* Structurally, civilization means a society in which individuals are tightly and complexly interrelated. It is an intense social life. Evaluatively, and as a consequence of the stimulation resulting from our more numerous and dense social relationships, civilization is also a higher degree of culture. In this chapter, I wish to address several threats to civil society in the United States: social distrust, political corruption, and cynicism.

SYMPTOMS OF AN UNCIVIL SOCIETY

Recent polls suggest that Americans are wary of other people, believe that morals have declined, and have little and declining trust in their institutions. In general terms, most people feel that others cannot be trusted and that lacks in common courtesy, respect, and a sense of responsibility are very significant problems in the United States.[2] Over three-fourths of U.S. adults believe that moral values are weak and that they have gotten weaker since the 1970s. Interestingly, more Americans choose the 1950s as the decade that contained the moral values that most closely reflect their own, and the 1990s as the time least representative of their own values.[3] Finally, with the possible exceptions of science and medicine, U.S. citizens do not have a lot of confidence in major institutions.[4] Among those most singled out for criticism are the federal government, the criminal justice system, the media, big business, and big labor. A large majority have only some or no confidence in them.[5] In a word, most simply do not trust these institutions.

Recent mega-scandals such as the savings-and-loan (S & L) crisis of the 1980s, involving both governmental botching and business fraud and incompetence, reinforce the distrust in major institutions. Estimates are that it will ultimately cost taxpayers $500 billion to $1.4 trillion to clean up the mess left by the scandal.[6] Briefly, this complicated debacle was set in motion by a series of events, most importantly the deregulation of savings-and-loan associations and raising of federal insurance on consumer depositors' money from $40,000 to $100,000.[7] The governmental action to allow these associations to increase the range and type of their investments, along with the increased security offered by higher insurance limits, created a situation that encouraged bankers to use their institutions' funds for get-rich-quick investments. While gambling with depositors' funds, bankers paid themselves and their employed family members handsomely. Greed, fraud, mismanagement, and stupidity combined to produce a monumental series of bad investments that caused many financial institutions to go bankrupt. In the aftermath, governmental officials sometimes actually stepped in to defend some of the worst offenders, and the government (i.e., taxpayers) was left to bail the institutions out of the whole mess.

The government's involvement in the S & L crisis reinforced its negative image. When compared to other institutions, confidence in the federal government has gone down relatively and absolutely since the early 1970s. Whether the government has become more corrupt or less effective, in fact, is still an open question. "Politics in the United States has long had a reputation for sleaze" going back at least to the early nineteenth century.[8] Since the 1960s, the media have certainly become more fully involved in publicizing details about governmental antics, so it is unclear whether the upward trend in public dissatisfaction is due more to an actual increase in wrongdoing by officeholders or to impressions created by the media. In any case, there is little doubt that public attitudes about institutions are decidedly negative. Regarding the recent investigation into campaign finance corruption, most do not believe that hearings will produce any new information and believe that both parties used unethical tactics to raise money.[9] Frequent stories about influence peddling by large political donors and private contractors do little to reinforce the public's belief in the fairness of the system. This ho-hum, cynical view of politics demonstrates, in part, the distance that has grown between government and politics and the everyday lives of most citizens.

The vast majority of U.S. adults simply do not believe that public officials care about the average person. "Despite the forms of greater democratic openness in the system (in fact often because of them), policymaking in the postmodern era revolves around contending bodies of activists who are largely detached from the bulk of ordinary citizens."[10] Ordinary citizens see each group of activists claiming that truth and morality is on their side. This only adds to the feelings of meaninglessness, lack of control, and inefficacy among the public. "The gap between policy activists and what have been called those with a commitment to everyday life is an equal-opportunity destroyer of public confidence, applying to the right and left of the political spectrum."[11]

The nastiness and bickering in politics at the national level is found on the local level, as well, as these examples show:

■ During a fiery debate on financing education, the president of the school board here [Rockford, IL] recently chose a rather dramatic way to express his disagreement with a fellow board member. He grabbed him by the throat....

■ In Lake Forest, Ill., a fairy-tale setting famous for its estates and high-tea etiquette, disagreements over Town Council decisions have led to smashed mailboxes and obscene telephone calls.

■ And in Arizona, a tax protester shot and wounded a Maricopa County Supervisor.[12]

In all these debates, truth seems unclear and far away. As one commentator put it, "Americans may no longer be so concerned with truth or it may be that so much truth is available everyone can have his own."[13] The average person does not have the skills or time to assess the claims being advanced by all contenders. Sometimes the truth does not even seem to matter. Consider what happens to whistle-blowers, individuals who believe that it is important to tell the truth and expose problems or dishonesty when it can have a significant effect on many people. It is not unusual for them to lose their jobs and have difficulty finding another one because they have been labeled troublemakers, malcontents, loose cannons, and misfits.[14]

All of this uncertainty, confusion, and suppression of truth may be the result of increasing centralization of power, corruption, and selfishness in society. Or they may be offsprings of the rapidity of social, political, and economic change, and the glut of information, opinion, and innuendo being poured out daily in the media. Or they may simply be the result of the proliferation of groups who want their voices heard (i.e., openness and democracy in action). Regardless of what causes of our current malaise are most significant, I want to make it clear that this does not mean that there are no immediate positive results from *some* of them. Some of these sources have mixed effects on citizenship. Newspapers, for example, although scorned publicly, provide many with information about social and political issues, and this exposure strengthens readers' ties to and involvement in their communities.[15] Similarly, we should expect that social pluralism in a democracy will rightly create demands by disparate groups for representation of their separate interests. Nevertheless, when trust and confidence are displaced by distrust and cynicism, this does not bode well for the prospects of a civil society.

UNRAVELING THE ROOTS OF POLITICAL CORRUPTION

What accounts for the corruption found in institutions that are supposed to serve the common good? Commentators have suggested everything from declines in values and consciences to family breakdowns, economic competition, pluralism, and wholesale shifts in institutional structures. Having been concerned with the ties among individuals and between them and institutions, the classical theorists addressed what they thought were the bases of attitudes and "consciousness" as well as behavior.

The term *moral* probably appears in the work of Durkheim more often than in the works by the others. He was undoubtedly concerned with matters of citizenship, governmental responsibilities, and selfishness in modern society. Recall that Durkheim viewed people as having a dual human nature, part instinctive, organic, and egoistic, and part moral, mental, and social. These elements are in an eternal war within us, one that he thought would intensify as civilization progressed. There seems to be little doubt that Durkheim considered the latter component to be the more worthy part of our natures. One facile explanation of corruption and distrust is simply to impute them to the animal side of our natures. It is painful to ignore this side of ourselves: "We cannot follow one of our two natures without causing the other to suffer."[16] Indeed, one of the most common sets of explanations for political corruption places the blame on the individual's faulty moral character.[17] But Durkheim reminded us that both sides of our selves are natural, and that it is the social structure of society that affects the fuller development of one side or the other.

We should never expect to get rid of all deviance. A certain amount of deviance is to be expected, and its normal rate is directly tied to the manner in which a society is organized. A society's social structure (a social fact) will generate deviance at a particular rate (another social fact). The fact is that our political structure and legislation on campaign contributions allow and sometimes encourage undue influence by the economically powerful, and thus create an opportunity and temptation for a given amount of political corruption. So if we are to change a rate of deviance and individuals' likelihood of committing it, we must change the social arrangements within the society. Durkheim, for example, argued that it is a mistake for us to view the social organization of the family as a product of individual human feelings; rather it is the other way around: "It is the social organization of the relations of kinship which has determined the respective sentiments of parents and children.... Everything that is found in [individual consciences] comes from society."[18] The division of labor and corporate groups, for example, necessitate our dependence on one another and thereby nurture the social and moral side of our natures. This means that if we did not live in society, we could not be moral. Eliminate society and you eliminate morality, for it is from society that we receive the moral content for our thinking.

The important point here is that Durkheim believed that society has to exist within the individual for its hold to be effective. Although society exists as a social fact outside the individual, it is having society *inside* the individual that curbs the egoistic side of our natures and promotes our need to take others into account before behaving. It is how the collective conscience of society becomes a guide for a meaningful and productive, though constrained, life.

How does a force that is outside get inside the individual? How do we get morality into the individual? Clearly, social arrangements that bring people together or create interdependence encourage an awareness and understanding of others. Social gatherings to celebrate important events in a society, working together, and being members of associations are significant for this purpose. They are seedbeds for the development of collective representations and the collective conscience. In addition, education is critical. Durkheim wrote extensively on the importance of moral education in young people. Since education is viewed by many as the master solution to most social problems, I will discuss Durkheim's argument about the relationship between morality and education in detail.

The Role of Education

Durkheim argued that **moral behavior** has certain characteristics. First, such behavior is consistent or regular (i.e., the person does not do something different every time or act unpredictably). Second, the behavior is carried out under a sense of obligation (i.e., there is a sense of authority implicit in the behavior; it is not done wantonly or selfishly, and it requires obedience to a norm outside the individual). For an act to be moral, we must do it because we *ought* to, out of respect for a moral precept, rather than because we may be punished if we do not do it. These two aspects mean that moral behavior requires *discipline*. Such discipline makes both social order and a meaningful goal-oriented existence for the individual possible. Chaos and lack of control over one's life results when such regulation is absent: All life requires "determinate rules, and to neglect them is to invite serious disturbance."[19] A lack of limitations and the encouragement of limitless horizons only invites a sense of disillusion, futility, and, ultimately, pessimism. This is a "malady of infinite aspiration," a "drowning in the dissolving sense of limitlessness."[20] It is expected, of course, that limitations will vary over time and place and over the lifetime of the individual.

In addition to entailing discipline, Durkheim believed that moral behavior is *impersonal* in nature (i.e., moral behavior is oriented toward the collectivity and reflects its interests rather than those of the individual). Morality is never self-oriented; it reinforces our attachment to the group: "Moral goals . . . are those the object of which is *society*. To act morally is to act in terms of the collective interest."[21] Durkheim stressed again the necessary interdependence of the individual and society. We are largely a product of society and become better because of our attachment to it: "Just as our physical organism gets its nourishment outside itself, so our mental organism feeds itself on ideas, sentiments, and practices that come to us from society."[22] As we saw in his analysis of egoistic suicide, we become more vulnerable when we are detached from the collectivity. We also become more selfish.

Finally, moral behavior must also be *autonomous* (i.e., it must be freely and rationally chosen by the individual on the basis of knowledge of alternative ways of behaving). The person voluntarily accepts the limitations imposed by society. As we gain in understanding our connections with others and why we need to act as we do, we also gain the autonomy required in a genuine and complete moral being. In relation to the problem of political corruption, one explanation is that some individuals do not have the discipline and sense of social obligation within them to act in a moral fashion. For Durkheim, it is the responsibility of society's institutions, principally its educational system, to create moral individuals.

Keep in mind that Durkheim is not talking about some narrow kind of religious morality, but rather a broader rational and secular morality. This is consistent with the manner in which society has evolved, from a focus on the supernatural to one on humankind. Morality has become more earthbound, as have religions, by stressing the centrality of love for our neighbor. The necessity of a morality that encompasses everyone becomes more obvious as artificial boundaries between nations fall and relationships within broad social structures increasingly tie together more people from different parts of the world.

The teaching of such morality must begin early. The period when children go to elementary school is the "critical moment in the formation of moral character."[23] If the foundations of morality are not laid then, they never will be. It is the school rather than the family that is most important for teaching morality as it relates to the demands of society. The morality that needs to be taught is one that focuses on the basics of our relations with others—more specifically, on the disposition of rights and obligations, and the justice and injustice within them.

To be effective in developing morality within children, teachers must feel the moral authority and importance of social norms themselves, must demand respect, and must use punishment judiciously. From Durkheim's perspective, two of the problems with many of our school systems today is that (1) teachers are under stress to accommodate parental demands for their children and (2) teachers often have trouble commanding respect in the classroom. In the mid-1990s, surveys suggest that a majority of parents have only some or little confidence in the educational system.[24] Parents demand special treatment for their children or question the grades meted out by teachers. When this happens, their focus is on themselves and their own children rather than children and society in general. This only serves to undermine the authority of teachers and the selfless orientation required in moral behavior.

Teacher authority can also be undermined by their own amoral or immoral behavior and media attention to it, thereby weakening respect for teachers. The larger size, greater heterogeneity, and competitive spirit of classrooms also make the instilling of respect for teachers more difficult to attain. At the same time, the varying cultural standards with which a multiethnic student group identifies might also diminish teacher authority, a fact that does not appear to have been fully appreciated by Durkheim.

Since the consciousnesses of children are relatively simple and narrow compared to those of adults, according to Durkheim, their consciousnesses must be broadened to increase their feelings of attachment to others. This can be accomplished by making them aware of the groups to which they belong, repeating this, and then encouraging group activity. Planting the idea must be reinforced by actual behavior, and the school, with its impersonal and group character, is the perfect place to initiate this attachment to others. The teacher can use the class to instill common ideas, feelings, and responsibilities. Durkheim might suggest more classroom activities that require a division of labor and the cooperation of everyone for the accomplishment of set goals.

In surveys cited earlier, it was found that the vast majority of Americans feel that morality has declined and needs to be strengthened. For Durkheim, the moral education of children is one way for maximizing the chances that, when they are adults, they will not act out of self-interest but out of recognition of society's norms. This would help minimize the extent of political corruption. If individuals are educated in morality, their behavior will be predictable because their actions will be disciplined. In addition, they will act in a normative way; their behavior will be consistent with the values of society because in their thoughts they are attached and responsible to society. This will reinforce the trust that is needed to cement stable social relationships. When respondents in a survey say that they cannot trust anyone, a large part of what they mean is that (1) people cannot be relied or depended on (i.e., their behavior is not predictable) and (2) people act out of self-interest rather than social interest.

Bureaucracy, Capitalism, and Corruption

A moral education introduces fundamental social values into a person's behavior, and may consequently curb corrupt behavior. When Weber bemoaned the lack of substantive rationality in modern society, he meant that social actions were seldom motivated by some ultimate set of humane values. Rather, people in modern society act as they do because the rules that prescribe their actions more often than not endorse that behavior which allows one to reach a defined end most efficiently, regardless of the nature of that end or the morality of the means. Part of the reason for this emphasis is the dominance of the bureaucratic form. Like Kafkaesque automatons, bureaucrats carry out their duties without thinking. They simply follow the rules without considering the human or other consequences of their behaviors.

In Weber's view, the bureaucratic form became prominent in modern capitalist society because it is more efficient, stable, and impersonal than **patrimonial** or **charismatic** forms of **organization.** As a relentless machine, the bureaucratic form can produce a given outcome better, more reliably, and more quickly than other forms, regardless of the outcome involved. State bureaucracy is also, and above all, an instrument of power, which, once in place, is virtually impossible to eliminate. This means that whoever controls it has a formidable weapon at their disposal. In contrast to Durkheim's belief that the modern state in a democracy exists to protect the freedom of the individual, Weber was aware that it can be put to any use for which one wants to use it. As such, it could be a *liberating* as well as an *oppressive* force. It is impersonal. Its neutrality in this regard makes it available for corrupt, self-interested uses as well as more publicly useful functions. Thus, a corrupt government *as a whole institution* is made possible by the lack of attachment of bureaucracy to any particular group or set of values.

Ironically, Weber viewed bureaucracy's impersonality also as a way of preventing corrupt and unethical behavior by *individuals*. Several of bureaucracy's characteristics are aimed at protecting individuals from abuse by those in authority and preventing use of a bureaucracy's resources for private gain. In the ideal-typical bureaucracy, the rules and responsibilities of positions are strictly defined, placement is based on technical expertise, and the authority and rights attached to positions are clearly delimited. A distinction is also made between private and organizational property. These features, if carried out, prevent abuses by individuals and clarify what it is one can and cannot do. According to Weber,

> Bureaucratization offers above all the optimum possibility for carrying through the principle of specializing administrative functions according to purely objective considerations.... "Objective" discharge of business primarily means a discharge of business according to calculable rules, "without regard for persons.".... Bureaucracy develops the more perfectly the more it is "dehumanized," the more completely it succeeds in eliminating from official business love, hatred, and all purely personal, irrational, and emotional elements which escape calculation.[25]

This means that it is when state organizations are *not* bureaucratic that individuals here and there are most likely to engage in corrupt behavior.[26] Real governments are never purely bureaucratic, of course. They contain mixtures of bureaucratic, patrimonial, and charismatic elements. When organizations are structured primarily in a patrimonial manner (i.e., when duties, rights, positions, and rules are not well defined or are broadly defined), a wide range of behavior is permissible. Tradition and custom hold more sway than formal written rules. Authority and behavior are more arbitrary. The leeway allows individuals to develop attachments to other *individuals* rather than to *positions*. Objectivity breaks down, and loyalty and favoritism rather than adherence to objective rules become more important as bases for behavior. The granting of personal favors, bribes, and the infusion of narrow group interests in legislation is more likely under patrimonial conditions. In essence, to the extent that political corruption means using power or position for personal gain, it is less likely if the state strictly follows bureaucratic principles. The presence of corruption by individuals would suggest that positions, rules, authority limitations, and distinctions between what belongs to the individual incumbent and what belongs to the state need to be more clearly defined and made known to officeholders. It is important to distinguish between a corrupt *government* and corrupt *individuals*. Bureaucracy reduces the chances of the latter but is no guarantee against the former.

Formal and substantive capitalist influences can easily infiltrate the state bureaucracy and use its power for capitalist ends. On the *formal* side, the very impersonality, objectivity, and machinelike character of bureaucracy makes it fit very nicely with capitalism, with which it shares those qualities. There is an "elective affinity" between them. "Today, it is primarily the capitalist market economy which demands that the official business of public administration be discharged precisely, unambiguously, continuously, and with as much speed as possible. Normally, the very large modern capitalist enterprises are themselves unequalled models of strict bureaucratic organization."[27] Through its issuance and control of a monetary system and its legislation, the state provides a stable environment within which capitalism can operate impersonally and efficiently. "Without regard for persons" is a watchword of capitalism as well as bureaucracy. As an ideal type, the capitalist organization will lay off employees, transfer jobs, and shut down plants to maintain the efficiency (of its means) to its end (profit). Like bureaucracy, it is soulless. The neutral character of bureaucracy, coupled with its close connection with capitalism, make state bureaucracy more vulnerable to the whims of capitalism.

On the *substantive* side, to the extent that state bureaucracy is a weapon at the disposal of anyone, one would assume that those who are most powerful would be most likely to wrest control of it. Like a prostitute, it is available to the highest bidder "without regard for persons." Once it is in place, bureaucracy "is easily made to work for anybody who knows how to gain control over it.... In modern times bureaucratization and social leveling within political...state organizations...have very frequently benefited the interests of capitalism. Often bureaucratization has been carried out in direct alliance with capitalist interests."[28] This does not mean that the state bureaucracy will necessarily serve the interests of capitalism, but that its impersonal nature makes it available to serve the interests of a variety of masters: "In this respect, one has to remember that bureaucracy as such is a precision instrument which can put itself at the disposal of quite varied—purely political as well as purely economic, or any other sort—of interests in domination."[29] It is democratic in this sense, but not necessarily democratic in the sense of government of the people, by the people, for the people. Average people do not make up a significant proportion of the federal government, and this lack of direct membership reduces their trust in it.[30]

If there is a good chance that state bureaucracy is influenced by capitalism, there is also a reasonable probability that political power will rest on economic power. Indeed, Weber contends that political power is frequently based on economic power in modern capitalist society. Weber was well aware of the influence of wealthy "party donors" on bureaucratic parties and political policy, especially in the United States.[31] As we know from recent disputes in the Congress, campaign financing from soft money and its influence on governmental policies has become a contentious issue as an increasing number of improprieties have been uncovered. Money has infected political election and policy processes extensively. It is very expensive to run for a national office. In the early 1990s, the cost of a successful Senate campaign was about $4,000,000.[32]

An obvious way to interpret this is to argue that to have significant political power, one needs economic power. There is much agreement between Weber and Marx on this point. As discussed earlier, Marx contended that the bourgeoisie, as owners of the means of production in capitalist society, were also the most politically powerful. They are a ruling class because as part of the **superstructure** of society, the political institution is predominantly influenced by the structure of relationships in the economic substructure. When some suggest that we need to "follow the money trail" to understand the process and content of political decision making, they are essentially proposing a Marxian analysis. The economic and political systems are also tied together because, on the one hand, the government depends on the revenues that result from the workings of the capitalist economic system, while on the other hand, the growth of capitalism requires the protection afforded by a stable and powerful central government. So regardless of who is in office, the structural connections between the two systems require that they support each other.

THE MISANTHROPIC TENDENCY

When money buys elections, bureaucracy seems intractable, education is ineffective, and firm moral guidelines appear to be absent in society, it is easy to see why so many people are cynical or distrustful of others and their institutions. Weber and Marx were both concerned with the dynamics of capitalism and the impact of economic power on the rest of society. Simmel, too, attempted to reveal the spirit of modern democratic society. In *The Philosophy of Money,* a study that his good friend Weber described as "simply brilliant," Simmel dissected the formal properties of money and their consequences. But he was less concerned with economic than with their cultural and psychological effects.

Money Talks

As is typical of his perspective, Simmel saw that money has both positive and negative consequences. On the positive side, it enhances one's freedom to express life as one wishes. In this sense, it supports individuality and thereby expands the complexity and richness of social life. Its possession also allows people to create a personal protective boundary against the demands and onrush of stimulation from city life. The positive impacts of money need to be kept in mind because the popular social-scientific view has been to stress the negative effects that flow from the nature and dominance of money in modern society. In her recent analysis of the social meaning of money, Viviana Zelizer criticizes not only the lack of attention that the social implications of money have received by sociologists but also the tendency to see it in a largely negative light.[33] In contrast, she stresses that there are different kinds of monies that can be used in different ways in social relationships. Informal monies (objects that can be exchanged for other objects) are involved in exchange, just like official money. Money can be earmarked for different uses, and in this sense, some money may be considered more important or honorable than other. Monies earmarked for welfare, charity, children, pleasure, and so on are thought of differently.

Whereas Zelizer's discussion broadens and deepens our understanding of the role of money, it seems to me that Simmel's analysis of official money remains intact because of his own admission and illustration that money has both positive and negative effects, and its universality allows it to be used by anyone for anything. The very properties of money that create social and psychological distance between people can bring them together in economic exchanges. One of the most important of money's properties is that it eliminates the qualitative differences among objects and reduces them to measurement on a single quantitative scale. In modern society, money tends to become a universal exchange medium. It has no allegiances or morality, it is distant "from all that is specific and one-sided," and because of this, it can be used by anyone for good or ill in society.[34]

Everything has a price tag, and that price is defined in terms of money. "For the cynical disposition, . . . everything and everybody is purchasable."[35] This undermines belief in real qualitative differences between things; everything can be measured in terms of its economic cost. Because money becomes a common measure, it is "the absolutely commensurate expression and equivalent of all values . . . it becomes the centre in which the most estranged and the most distant things find their common denominator."[36] When the qualitative differences in value between objects become reduced to differences in money, it means a price tag can be placed on anything. This in turn breeds cynicism.

Cynicism is "almost endemic to the heights of a money culture" and results from "the reduction of the concrete values of life to the mediating value of money."[37] What is of real value is diminished because of its measurement in terms of mere grubby money. This condition informs the cynic's view of life and what makes the world go around: "His [the cynic's] awareness of life is adequately expressed only when he has theoretically and practically exemplified the baseness of the highest values and the illusion of any differences in values."[38] What even further deepens these beliefs is that every day the cynic sees that on a massive scale "the finest, most ideal and most personal goods are available not only for anyone who has the necessary money, but even, more significantly, where these goods are denied to the most worthy if he lacks the necessary means."[39] Innumerable, rapid, daily monetary transfers on the stock exchange demonstrate the centrality of money as the bottom line in the shifting of goods. On the one hand, money allows us to put our values into practice. But on the other hand, if money is the main way by which we can externalize our values, this means that it is money, not virtue or value, that makes the world what it is.

The Push for Profit

Marx also viewed money as making the world go around. Owners are in business to make a profit, and anything legal that increases profit is acceptable. In his discussions of capitalism's stages, in every case, alterations are made to drive up profit. In the early stages of capitalism's development, free workers are brought together under one roof to produce goods for the factory owner. The more workers, the greater the profit. Later, simultaneously to drive down the cost of inefficiency and increase the bottom line, capitalists introduced a detailed division of labor among workers. Then, to lower the cost of labor, machines took the place of an increasing number of employees. The fundamental point is that capitalists act primarily on the basis of an economic motive.

Recent economic disruptions in the form of corporate closings, layoffs, transfers, and mergers are aimed at increasing efficiency, maximizing competitiveness, and enhancing profit. The objections of affected employees more often than not are futile. In their attempts to stop or stall these major shifts, unions have lost more battles than they have won. Few workers expect to stay in the same jobs they are in now; most expect some mobility, even if it is not voluntary. The uncertainty created by this situation breeds wariness and skepticism among employees. It also reduces attachment to employers, which in turn means greater distrust. In employers' attempts to reduce costs, the hiring of nonunion workers, the reduction of fringe benefits such as health care, and the demands for employees to work longer hours expands the alienation between workers and employers. What is viewed as exploitation weakens the trust between them. Shifts in the occupational structure leave some workers adrift as the skills upon which they relied to make their living no longer apply in the new occupations. This creates further uncertainty. Recent research has indeed found a link between economic shifts and uncertainty on the one hand, and incivility on the other.[40]

When significant changes occur in the economy, such as mergers or plant layoffs, employers usually publicize a statement explaining how their actions are for the good of the country (e.g., to improve the balance of trade), or the company (e.g., to be able to compete internationally), or the workers (e.g., to increase demand and thus create new jobs). For Marx, this is merely an ideology designed to justify actions in which the only material interest being considered is that of the company's profit. Part of the reason average citizens become cynical about such statements is that ours is a country that has extolled individualism, so it is easy to believe that everyone is out for themselves. At the same time, as a democracy, we are supposed to engage in activities that promote the common good, as well. In the clash between beliefs in individualism and the common good, people become cynical when behavior in the name of one really masks behavior being done for the other:

> [A] perpetual cynicism is produced and reproduced in democracies because the necessary balancing act between individual interests and the common good provokes suspicions and differences in judgment. People suspect that actions in the name of the public good actually serve individual private interests. Thus the notion that politicians are all corrupt, that they are all "in it for themselves," is a recurring theme of American political discourse.[41]

"Well Whatever"

Cynicism and distrust are also fed by a cultural system whose values are so broad as to be meaningless or whose values and guidelines for behavior lack legitimacy. Earlier I reviewed surveys that revealed a widespread belief that Americans lack a firm and common morality. In its absence, people cannot be trusted to act for the other person's good, but only for themselves. In the absence of a concern for the public good, political corruption is also more likely. Weber believed that as capitalism had established itself, the religious roots of the capitalist spirit had become less important, being replaced by a secular ethic that served the economic system. The religious asceticism out of which the capitalist spirit arose stressed that we should not be too personally attached to wealth, since it is because of God's grace that we have obtained it. When wealth was accumulated by the capitalists, it was to be used for the greater glory of God, not for private luxury. Individuals were to be stewards rather than exploiters of their wealth. The Protestant ethic was important then, in part because it caused us to develop a moral relationship with society in general. Without that element, wealth poses a serious temptation and danger to the individual and morality. This diminution of the moral element in economic actions lends itself to the greater manipulation of others for personal gain.

Durkheim was adamant that when a general set of guiding values and norms is absent or ineffective, society is set adrift. Anything goes. What does one do? How does one act? "Well whatever" is the response. Whatever it takes. Durkheim believed that a person must be bound by "a conscience superior to his own, the superiority of which he feels."[42] This "regulative force" present in society, when effective, restrains the individual's passions, consequently ensuring that individuals will not be subject to the disappointments and frustration that come from a lack of goals and limits. "But when society is disturbed by some painful crisis or by beneficent but abrupt transitions, it is momentarily incapable of exercising this influence."[43]

It is the change itself, not whether it is positive or negative, that brings about disorganization of the existing social and normative order. Rapid and drastic changes upset established arrangements and rules within society without new "just" arrangements being in place. The development of a new regulatory system takes time and is not a matter of simply sitting down and developing a new philosophy of life. A new moral code "can arise only through itself, little by little, under the pressure of internal causes which make it necessary."[44] In the meantime, the result is *anomie,* a bewildering situation in which there is no effective set of moral guidelines. This social and cultural condition of malaise manifests itself in the psychological state of the individuals subject to it. Those exposed to anomie experience a sense of limitlessness and no restraints; their emotions and passions are overextended. Having no limits, they feel no sense of accomplishment, no feeling of reaching a goal, of going anywhere. Durkheim described them as suffering from an "infinity of desires."[45] Agitation, torment, and a sense of never being satisfied results.

Socially, the malintegration of different parts of society results in disharmony and waste.[46] As a result, the social structure is not a just one. *Culturally,* the lack of societal restraints means that individuals are not being guided morally; thus, they are not sensitive of their obligations to others. Durkheim believed that modern Western society is going through a period of anomie on its way to a more harmonious, just society. The egoistic individualism, moral confusion, and injustice found in an anomic society readily lend themselves to the growth of interpersonal distrust, cynicism, and corruption. An anomic state also suggests many of the features that have been attributed to a postmodern society and culture. Rapid change, the absence of fixed truth, excessive individuality, the ineffectiveness of grand explanations, and constant activity and stimulation are all found in anomic societies. Anomie may also provide us with a possible understanding of the various social, cultural, and religious groups whose members are seeking meaning and direction in life, and a way of relating morally to others.

When relationships among individuals are either absent, unjust, or disturbed, effective common assemblies among them are rare. Since, according to Durkheim, it is in such social gatherings that the collective ideas and force are born, the collective conscience that restrains individuals cannot fully develop. Without this assembly, collective ideals become problematic and the sacred elements of life remain dormant: "Society cannot make its influence felt unless it is in action, and it is not in action unless the individuals who compose it are assembled together and act in common."[47] Collective ideas and sentiments receive their life and existence from collective *actions*. All aspects of the sacred part of life—ideals, morals, concepts, knowledge, symbols—arise from collective life. If people separate themselves from each other, they cannot be stimulated and common values cannot be reinforced. Such assemblies allow us to rise out of and above ourselves, to be a part of something greater. This is what makes national holidays and parades so important. They reinforce the civil religion of what it means to be a U.S. citizen. Experiencing rituals with others makes one feel stronger (e.g., witness the fervor of the Promise Keepers when assembled, or even a pep rally).

Unfortunately, when anomie exists, the old ideas and established assemblies may no longer move as many as they once did. New ideas and assemblies are needed for a moral order that is consistent with the social changes that are occurring. Cynicism and matter-of-factness in society suggest the absence of a collective base and a lack of society in the individual. For the individual to be civilized, he or she must have the knowledge, language, morality, and technology that can come only from society. The widespread lack of civility indicates that society is not enough in us.

CONCLUSION

As Comparative Chart 5.1 indicates, there are numerous arguments and ideas in classical theories to help account for the recent divisive prevalence of political corruption, cynicism, and distrust in the United States. Many of these intersect with each other. Culturally, the impersonality and amorality of capitalism and bureaucracy do little to create a moral framework by which to live, and the infiltration of money as a central dimension of many relationships often discourages the development of social bonds based on enduring humane values. Although it connects us with others and frees us to express our individuality, money also distances us from objects and others and creates attachments that are, at best, shal-

COMPARATIVE CHART 5.1   Basic Ideas from Each Theorist Used in Analyses of Chapter Issues

	Political Corruption	Misanthropic Tendency
Marx	Economic power as basis of political power; interdependence of government and economy	Profit as the basis for evolution in capitalism and distrust; effectiveness of ideology as tool to justify economic policies
Durkheim	Human nature inadequate explanation of corruption; deviance rates linked to type of social structure; need for society to be internalized; nature of morality and its need for nurturance by teachers in early education	Anomie as a condition of absence of moral regulation; lack of collective assemblies weakens collective conscience
Simmel		Money as fostering individuality; money as universal medium of exchange eliminating qualitative differences; money as basis for cynicism
Weber	Dominance of rational action and bureaucratic form as connected to corruption; bureaucracy as inhibitor of personal corrupt behavior; superiority of bureaucracy over patrimonial and charismatic forms; affinity between bureaucracy and capitalism creating vulnerability to corruption; economic power corrupting government	Secularization of capitalist spirit and exploitation of wealth

low in nature. When coupled with formal rationality and the lack of an encompassing set of moral guidelines, it foments callousness and egoism. Structurally, the interconnections between political and economic power leave many feeling either powerless or cynical, and create what Mills referred to as a "structural immorality." The intimate relationship between these institutions invites political corruption. Finally, continuous and dramatic changes in broad social-structural connections help disintegrate established moral systems, without leaving any replacement in their wake. This leaves individuals with little stability or direction in their lives, encouraging selfishness, distrust, and cynicism. Unfortunately and paradoxically, while partially a product of individualism, cynicism ultimately undermines our sense of efficacy and renders us powerless. In this way, it is a long-term threat to democracy.[48]

It is important to remember that although the classical theorists provided us with clues as to the sources of the kinds of problems being discussed here, they also discussed many of the integrative effects that can arise from the cultural and social conditions of modern society. For example, despite its deficiencies, both Simmel and Weber preferred competitive capitalism to what they felt was the overpowering oppressiveness of socialism. Bureaucracy is impersonal, but its very impersonality demands that everyone be treated according to the same standards. In this sense, it encourages fairness and justice. Money can corrupt, but it is also a means of freedom and the realization of dreams.

Finally, the classical theorists' perspectives help us understand the bases of corruption and cynicism, but they leave some questions unanswered. One issue not anticipated by Durkheim, for example, is whether *physical* presence is necessary for assemblies to be effective, or is "presence" in any sense of the term just as meaningful? Does watching Princess Diana's entire funeral on TV have the same collective impact as actually attending it? This relates to the issues of community raised earlier in Chapter 3. Weber noted that the state bureaucracy can serve any master. But is there a way to ensure that the bureaucratic state devises policies that serve everyone rather than a select few? Marx described the incestuous relationship between political and economic interests. But is it possible to get money out of politics and still get the best candidates elected? Simmel's masterwork was on the impact of money on society, culture, and the individual. But how can we minimize its insidious corrosive effects and still retain its utility? Money is certainly intimately involved in the exchange of commodities and in the creation of individuals as commodities. This is the subject I will explore in Chapter 6.

QUESTIONS TO PONDER

1. What do you think are the relative roles of the family and school in promoting moral (i.e., uncorrupted selfless) behavior? Is Durkheim's emphasis on the school misplaced? Explain.

2. If capitalism encourages a maximization of personal profit, can moral behavior ever be maximized without changing the structure of capitalism?

3. As a universal medium of exchange, Simmel linked money to cynicism in society. Was he right to do so? Why or why not? If you agree with Simmel, how can money's effect in this regard be minimized?

CHAPTER 6

COMMODIFICATION AND THE VALUE OF HUMAN LIFE

CHAPTER IN BRIEF

- **INTRODUCTION**

materialism and concern for outward appearance; body, celebrity, and human life as commodities

- **THE SUPERFICIAL SELF**

extent of cosmetic surgery; gender and concern for attractiveness; historical shifts in beauty ideal; beauty ideal and women's roles; attractiveness and psychological traits; body and self-image; emotional labor and presentation of self; emotions and body as commodities; *Beauty as Cult and Body as Icon* (Durkheim): profane body as sacred; models as totems and symbolic representations of collective ideals; anorexia as denial of profane and exaltation of sacred; male origin of body ideal; *The Influence of Class and Capitalism* (Marx): class and access to cosmetic surgery; class and ideal body image; body parts as fetishes and commodities; exchange value of body parts; profit, beauty ideology, and sale of emotions

- **PEOPLE BOUGHT AND SOLD: THE WORLD OF CELEBRITIES**

athletes and celebrities as commodities; profit motive in sports; film stars and

building of celebrity status; presentation of celebrities as familiar and exceptional; television news celebrities and blurring of fact and fiction; *Capitalism in Entertainment* (Marx): stages of capitalism and phases in film industry; celebrity selling and ideological control; *Enchantment and Disenchantment of Celebrity* (Weber): rationalization and disenchantment of modern life alongside irrational charisma of celebrity; nature of charismatic authority; publicity bureaucracies and selling of celebrity; celebrities and selling of values

- **THE VALUE OF HUMAN LIFE**

importance of ultimate values; measures of the value of human life; value of human life and economic standing; *Rational Medicine and the Giving of Life* (Weber and Marx): rationalization of behavior of medical professionals; marketing of body parts; balancing quality of care and quantity of profit in medicine

INTRODUCTION

It has been said many times that ours is a materialistic culture. Implicit in this condemnation is the belief that wealth and social achievement are more important to many Americans than spiritual and moral values. The worth of individuals is generally measured in terms of their social and economic success and the lifestyle they present to the rest of society. How individuals look in outward appearance matters because it affects how others react to them. One consequence is that a great number of Americans are obsessed with their bodies. This concern over one's body can be warranted, of course, if it leads one to make changes that improve one's health. But too often, the obsession has little to do with health and everything to do with trying to fit a socially and culturally imposed ideal of what the body should look like.

In this chapter, I will deal with three ways in which the body is treated as a commodity in U.S. society. The first concerns what one author has dubbed "the cult of thinness"—that is, our relentless pursuit of the perfect body and our attempts to manufacture a pleasing physical presence. The second relates to how people are bought and sold as celebrity commodities. Individuals have varying dollar values on their heads and are considered either assets or debits. In the third section, I will move beyond a focus on the body and celebrity status and discuss the value of human life in general as a commodity and as portrayed in medicine. The common element in all three of these sections is an underlying concern for the multiple ways by which human life has been allegedly cheapened in contemporary U.S. society through treatment of the body as an object. The chapter continues the book's theme of separation and unity through its focus on the body as an object separate from the self. This approach to human life alienates individuals from each other and from themselves.

THE SUPERFICIAL SELF

To maintain a positive self-image, the presentation of self to others includes offering a physical and emotional self that is socially acceptable and status enhancing. Many Americans are willing to go to great lengths to manipulate, reshape, sculpt, and downright torture their bodies in order to present the ideal body to others. The American Academy of Cosmetic Surgery reported that 1.6 million people in the United States had various kinds of surgical reshaping done in 1994. These primarily included operations on those parts of the body that have the most direct influence on our social status (e.g., breasts, buttocks, hips, faces, and penises).[1] Liposuction and breast enlargement are the two most frequent kinds of cosmetic surgery.[2] In the early 1990s, it was estimated that $300 million was being spent yearly on cosmetic surgery. Single operations can range in cost from a few hundred dollars for a "chemical face peel" to $5,000 for a "tummy tuck." Added to these costs are the over $50 billion spent on cosmetics and diet remedies to present an attractive body.[3]

The concern for attractiveness has been associated more with females than with males. Traditionally in Western cultures, women have been viewed as more natural and emotional, and as a consequence, their identity has been more connected with their bodies than is the case with men, who have been thought to be more rational and intellectual than women.[4] Given this historical connection between women and the body, on the one hand, and men and the mind, on the other, it is not surprising that research suggests women have been more concerned than men with how they look and have been more likely to undergo cosmetic surgery.

The definition of *attractive* varies cross-culturally and across time.[5] Part of the reason for variations in the meaning of beauty relates to the fact that one's body image involves several dimensions and criteria. At a minimum, these concern evaluations of the body based on its skill or physical competence, its size and shape, and appearance as related to gender-specific functions (e.g., reproduction). The relative importance of each of these criteria can vary over time and between individuals. The ancient Greeks defined beauty in terms of proportionality and balance, whereas the Romans prized thinness and practiced systematic vomiting to prevent the gaining of excessive weight. During the periods of the late Middle Ages and early industrialization in Europe, a more rosy complexion and a plump, round, fertile-looking shape were admired. It was only near the beginning of the twentieth century that a thin female form was viewed as the ideal in the United States. After World War I, the more asexual, boyish shape with flattened breasts was the model of beauty to follow. A bustier, more shapely form was idealized in the 1940s and 1950s, with Betty Grable and Marilyn Monroe as beauty icons. But in the 1960s, thinness returned as the ideal, personified perhaps in the appearance of the fashion model Twiggy. Thinness has remained an ideal but, in contrast to the thinness that was advocated during the 1920s, it has also been associated with an acceleration in the number of eating disorders among U.S. women. In the 1980s, an image of ideal female beauty included an image of both thinness and strength (a "toned" body).

The shifts in beauty ideals involve changes in the focus on different body parts. The significance of the legs, bust, hips, buttocks, waist, and neck as the defining element of beauty has waxed and waned over time. These trends in the ideal image are tied to fluctuations in the social status, roles and functions of women in society at the time, and changes in technology and the economy. When women have been viewed primarily as mothers and wives (e.g, in the late 1940s and 1950s), their ideal body image is in tune with those functions. The women's revolution, rapid entrance of more women into the labor market, and stress on female independence of the 1960s implied a different, thinner image, not as attractive to males. Nevertheless, patriarchal forces in society still place a heavy push on women to shape their bodies to fit the male ideal of female beauty. What is defined as the model of attractiveness is also linked to the class position and race of women. I will say more later about the social, cultural, political, and economic factors behind beauty ideals.

One indication of the importance placed on attractiveness in U.S. society is the extent to which people tie it to other positive attributes. Attractive people are simply viewed in a more favorable light than others. Research suggests that beautiful people are thought by many to be more self-confident, likeable, successful, warmer, happier, smarter, sociable, and competent than uglier people. These beliefs are most likely to be held by those who are especially sensitive to how they are viewed by others and who hold sex stereotypes about men and women. Others associate beauty with self-centeredness and adherence to gender-typical attitudes and behavior. For example, more so than unattractive females, beautiful women are thought to be infatuated with themselves and to display typically feminine traits.[6] Western history does reveal a paradoxical view of beautiful women. While placed on a pedestal and given homage, they are also seen as seductresses and temptresses, as weakeners of men.

Thomas Cash suggests that we have two images of ourselves, one from the outside and another from the inside, and that there is no necessary connection between them. "Beauty is no guarantee of a favorable body image, nor is homeliness a decree for a negative body image."[7] At the same time, we know that in the lifelong process of socialization, people learn to see themselves as others see them and to evaluate themselves on the basis of that appearance. Individuals see themselves as objects, looking at themselves from others' point of view, and assessing that appearance. The body is the most visible aspect of ourselves, and it is especially salient for women in U.S. society.[8] This means that how a woman physically presents herself reflects on her own self-image.

In addition to the body, being sensitive to how to present oneself also involves controlling the other physical aspects of the presentation. In other words, mannerisms, how one speaks, and the tone of voice, for example, need to be consciously crafted to fit the situation. As in the presentation of a particular body, this is important in the selling of oneself to others and to the maintenance of one's social status. But it too involves manipulation. Arlie Hochschild is generally credited with having the most famous study of the conscious presentation of manufactured emotions. Hochschild observed and interviewed employees at

Delta Airlines to find out how flight attendants were trained to present themselves to passengers. Attendants engage in what Hochschild dubbed "emotional labor," which "requires one to induce or suppress feeling in order to sustain the outward countenance that produces the proper state of mind in others."[9] The reference to "the outward countenance" means that the reaction conveying a sense of emotions to the passenger must be physically visible. As Hochschild indicates, such a display is a way of inducing the internal feelings in the passenger that one desires. Flight attendants may not necessarily really feel these emotions but to convey a sense that they do is critical for them to be effective in their roles. This emotional presentation is labor because it must be worked at; for instance, even if the attendant does not feel like smiling, she must smile and make it look genuine and natural. This is part of her job.

What happens in this case, as Hochschild describes it, is that the emotions and feelings, rather than being ways to find out about oneself, become a commercial resource used to satisfy customers and consequently raise profit. This "instrumental stance" toward the emotions is relatively new in our society, and makes it more difficult to realize what one really feels: "It is from feeling that we learn the self-relevance of what we see, remember, or imagine. Yet it is precisely this precious resource that is put in jeopardy when a company inserts a commercial purpose between a feeling and its interpretation."[10]

As I see it, what this economic use of emotions has in common with efforts to shape one's body into a socially and culturally acceptable form is that in both cases what is personal is treated as a commodity subject to rules that are externally rather than internally mandated. The emotional displays and body are manufactured to fit dominant ideas about what is appropriate. As Hochschild noted during her observations of flight-attendant training sessions, attendants are encouraged to view themselves as *selling their selves*. Cosmetic surgery is also an attempt to make oneself feel better because one will fit the culturally defined standard of what it means to be a beautiful woman. When a reshaped body effectively sells itself to admiring onlookers, one feels better about oneself. But it is a feeling dependent on the successful adherence to another's measure of beauty. Emotional labor and body shaping serve the same function here; they are designed to ensure compliance with a dominant standard. They are both part of the physical, alienated, and superficial presentation of self.

Beauty as Cult and Body as Icon

The alienation of the body and emotions from the feeling thinking self that is represented by cosmetic surgery and emotional labor parallels the dichotomy that has long been made between the mind and the body. Durkheim made such a distinction in separating the sacred from the profane. In his view, the **sacred** sphere of life incorporates all the higher elements of life: reason, morality, science, conceptualizations, impersonality (objectivity and unselfishness), altruism, holiness, and the soul. The **profane** level includes the more earthy aspects of life: sensations, body, materials, egoism, the personal, and the concrete. Durkheim viewed these two spheres as being in conflict with each other. Yet these worlds meet in the totem, which is a physical symbol or representation of a collective feeling or belief.

Durkheim was well aware that we cannot delimit what can be defined as sacred: "In a word, anything can be sacred."[11] Although Durkheim did not consider the body to be part of the sacred domain, ironically in our own time the body has become sacred, to the point of being adored if it meets the collective ideal of beauty. "Sacred things are simply collective ideals that have fixed themselves on material objects."[12] Models who fit this ideal have become totems or icons to whom we pay homage. They are idealizations of our highest standards of physical appearance and presentation. They are symbols of what many women themselves hope to be. Implicit in putting them on a pedestal is the notion that, because they are sacred, they are untouchable and separate from the rest of us mere mortals.

The high esteem and status that are given our model totems is ultimately rooted in the collective beliefs and feelings that arise from living together in a society. For Durkheim, it is social assembly that gives rise to shared ideas and ideals. Because these ideals arise in the presence of many, they are given the power and status of a moral force that dominates the individuals who are part of the group and who subscribe to them. This helps account for the lengths to which some will go to attain the perfect body: "When these ideals move our wills, we feel that we are being led, directed, and carried along by singular energies that, manifested, do not come from us but are imposed from the outside."[13]

Efforts to create the perfect body sometimes take a pathological direction. Catherine Garrett recently examined anorexia nervosa from a Durkheimian perspective.[14] She spoke with individuals who had suffered from this disorder and used their own words to analyze the meaning and process of anorexia. Participants in the study described their extreme fasting behavior as a kind of "spiritual quest" to connect more fully with themselves, others, and nature. In order to reach their goal of communion with all these elements, they felt a need to go through the "negative" phase of anorexia to reach the "positive" connections with themselves and their surroundings.

In discussing the opposition of the sacred and profane spheres of life, Durkheim asserted that one must give up all that is profane in order to reach spirituality. This means asceticism is necessary; suffering, abstinence, and discipline are required. Since our natural desire is to hold on to the profane world with its attendant indulgence in the physical senses, asceticism "cannot develop without causing suffering. Pain is one of its necessary conditions."[15] Abstinence has a sanctifying power. During these "negative rites," the body must be purged for the individual to reach a purified spiritual stage: "In general, all acts characteristic of the ordinary life are forbidden while those of the religious life are taking place. The act of eating is, of itself, profane. . . . This is why it is prohibited in religious times."[16] To effectively carry out this purifying asceticism, these abstaining practices "become the basis of a veritable scheme of life."[17]

Durkheim stressed that this rite of passage through the negative cult involving self-sacrifice and suffering is necessary to reach the positive cult involving a sense of connection with others. In this manner, asceticism becomes a way of controlling egoistic tendencies and rising above ourselves. For society to survive, self-sacrifices are necessary: "Society itself is possible only at this price."[18] There are times when the negative rites become an end in themselves and do not evolve into a more positive phase, which is basically what happens when anorexics do not recover but simply continue their ascetic self-deprivation. At this point, writes Durkheim, the negative rite "exaggerates itself to the point of usurping the entire existence . . . [it becomes] a hypertrophy of the negative cult."[19]

As pointed out earlier, anorexics in Garrett's study defined their negative, depriving behavior as part of a spiritual quest whose positive goal is a deep feeling of relationship with themselves and the outside world. The attainment of connections created a feeling of spirituality, which meant a sense of oneness with all parts of the self (body, mind, soul), breaking down the artificial separation created between them during the fasting period when the mind and spirit try to control the body. Successful recovery meant an inner harmony was accomplished among these different components.

All attempts to reshape the body involve discipline, self-sacrifice, and hard work. Exercise, dieting, and elective surgery demand that we not give into our natural desire to sit around, eat, and do nothing. It is difficult to do these without support from others. Periodic rituals or meetings among believers help renew and strengthen these collective ideals. Weight watchers' meetings and aerobic classes, for example, in their own ways reinforce the ideals of the perfect body and encourage believers to keep the faith. Aerobic classes generally aim toward creating a body that is feminine yet firm, consistent with the 1980s beauty ideal mentioned earlier. Yet their members reveal an ambiguous attitude toward the ideal that reflects both their confusion about the ideal and suspicions about the social origins attributed to it by Durkheim.

One of the assumptions in Durkheim's argument here is that the ideal arises out of the collective activity and is further reinforced by such activity. Feminists argue that the ideal has arisen out of *male* collective activity in which females have had little role. The ideal body is a product of men, not women. Thus, women are trying to satisfy a shape created by a "male gaze." This is the origin of the ambivalence experienced by women who submit themselves to the demands of aerobic exercise. They object to the ideal but nevertheless continue to strive to attain it.[20] Although its origins may be collective, it is not an ideal created by women's collective consensus, as Durkheim might suggest. This is why it has been suggested that both capitalistic and patriarchal systems that support the thin ideal of beauty and do violence to women must be attacked.[21]

The Influence of Class and Capitalism

Marx argued that capitalism and the class structure within it shaped the lives of those living within them. The economic costs associated with elective surgery and the time costs involved in attending regular exercise and eating classes suggest that not everyone has an equal chance in attempting to reach the beauty ideal. To the extent that body image affects one's self-esteem and social acceptance, this means that social class deeply influences the extent to which individuals with varying resources can feel good about themselves and fit into the dominant society. Evidence indicates that different socioeconomic groups may have different images of beauty, but that the dominant thin ideal is infiltrating their value systems. Among African American women, the beautiful woman is fuller, softer, and more supple. Consequently, black women have been less likely to see themselves as overweight. As a group, African American women have not had the high rate of eating disorders found among white women. But as their incomes rise, so do their concerns about being thin and about meeting the other criteria associated with the dominant white ideal of beauty. This means that the natural features of many black women—wide noses, brown eyes, kinky hair, and the like—are vilified and make the ideal more difficult to attain.[22]

As Marx would suggest, what is valued in society more often than not reflects the interests and possessions of the upper class. The physical appearance of those in the upper class may be considered more attractive because of their wealth. Fussell even suggests that one's body profile and weight tend to be associated in popular culture with particular classes. Upper-class aristocrats are stereotyped as being tall, thin, and graceful, whereas working-class individuals are portrayed as heavy, stout, and more clumsy.[23] Thus, the cultural image has the upper class fitting the beauty ideal of thinness, while those in the lower classes have a long way to go. Ironically, the image of the upper-class woman as thin and delicate, juxtaposed with a belief in the working-class woman as more robust and sturdy, reinforce and even help justify the medical treatment received by the former while the latter were expected to be employed in hard, manual labor. In this way, attributed body images have served to perpetuate the class structure.

The beauty ideal is the ideal admired by those with socioeconomic power. And to be prized, it must be relatively rare. When others obtain it, its value lessens. It can no longer be used as effectively by the upper class as a means of distinguishing their position and lifestyle. Consequently, beauty ideals have shifted historically as those in the lower classes have been able to attain them. This was the case with the use of cosmetics after the First World War. Initially, only upper-class women could afford them. But as the cost became less prohibitive, women in the working and lower classes used cosmetics more, essentially cheapening them and reducing their effectiveness as an upper-class distinction. Consequently, upper-class women toned down their use of cosmetics, and excessive use of them became a sign that one was from the working class.[24] What this example suggests is that beauty is a social construction, an ideology based in the class system and deriving specifically from the upper class.

The focus in beauty ideals on particular parts of the body suggests that each one has become a commodity and a fetish. "A commodity," Marx wrote, "is, in the first place, an object outside us, a thing that by its properties satisfies human wants of some sort or another."[25] As commodities, body parts, especially those that are surgically altered, are also fetishes. They are seen as independent objects but really are manifestations of a set of social relationships in society. The relationships between patients and physicians, among physicians themselves, between purchasers and buyers, and between men and women in patriarchal society make up the real social relationships in this case. But the fetishism of commodities means that the relationships that are experienced are viewed as relationships between objects rather than individuals. If a physician can buy a BMW because of the tummy tucks he gives women, then, in a sense, the tucks represent and are related to the BMW. Tucks stand for a BMW. Instead of being a relationship between people, it is the objects they produce that are then related. It is as if the relationship between the products has an existence that is independent of the social and economic relationships between individuals.

In the preceding example, a refashioned body part is exchanged for an automobile. Commodities have both use value and exchange value. The *use* value of a commodity refers to its immediate utility to the owner. In addition to other uses, I use my car to drive to work; therefore, it has use value for me. *Exchange* value refers to the value of the commodity on the marketplace (i.e., what and how much can I get for it). I suggest that certain body parts that are enhanced, sculpted, reduced, firmed up, and so on, through cosmetic surgery can be effectively viewed as commodities whose exchange value can be increased through such surgery. Big breasts are worth something in the marketplace of our capitalistic and patriarchal culture. In most cases, the exchange values of the body parts associated with beauty outweigh their use values. In speaking of one's own body parts as commodities, and thereby featuring them as objects outside ourselves, as products for sale, it is also evident that a certain amount of alienation has occurred between these parts and ourselves. They are things rather than an integral part of who we are. This process is at the core of what Marx meant by alienation.

As products in the marketplace, bodies and their parts become exchanged within the capitalist system. The products and services that reshape bodies to increase their exchange value also become valued. This means that there is money to be made by companies that sell these products. Moreover, it is in their material interest to make sure that the effects that their products create continue to be valued. The profit of the manufacturer of diet pills goes up as the value of thinness increases in society. Ideology and capitalism work hand in hand here. Ideology increases profit, and profit can be used to reinforce beauty ideology.

The profit motive that drives capitalist interests applies to the selling of emotions, as well. As Hochschild's study demonstrates, customers must be satisfied if they are to return for more purchases. To do this, not only an attractive physical appearance but a pleasing emotional presentation must be given to customers. They are commodities that have a distinct exchange value in the competitive market. In this light, both the body and one's emotions are for sale.

PEOPLE BOUGHT AND SOLD:
THE WORLD OF CELEBRITIES

Attractive bodies are only one type of the many forms of marketplace commodities. At the higher ends of the wealth spectrum, professional athletes and popular celebrities also command a certain price in the market, and to the extent that they become thought of as objects of costs or profits, they are also commodities. It is these groups on which I will concentrate in this section.

The commodity character of athletes and celebrities is multidimensional. As commodities, professional athletes, for instance, command great salaries and, under certain rules, can be bought and sold. Professional sports is big business. In 1994, the average yearly salary of major league baseball players was $1,200,000. As a point of comparison, in 1931, Babe Ruth was paid $80,000 by the New York Yankees. In addition to the tens of millions of dollars in revenue from attendance, baseball also receives vast amounts from the television broadcast of games. The five-year contract negotiated with the Fox and NBC networks in 1995 was worth $1.7 billion. Baseball is not the only sport that is big business.

The average football player in the National Football League made $650,000 a year in 1994, and the average team took in over $39 million from TV broadcasts during the 1994–97 period:

> Professional players, teams, and leagues have a symbiotic relationship with the print and broadcast media, which are themselves compartmentalized into specialized units. Games receive extensive coverage in newspapers and magazines and are broadcast on radio and television. Income from consumers, who pay for the use of these services, and from advertisers, who sell their wares through the media, provides impetus to the commercialization of sports.[26]

When one considers that these figures do not include other professional sports such as basketball and hockey, or revenues from attendance and the sales of related merchandise, or revenues generated in businesses located in cities with such teams, it becomes even more obvious how economically powerful professional sports are.

The continued economic success of professional sports depends on its popularity with the public. In the first half of the twentieth century, baseball players generally did not earn a lot of money; a stronger motivation to play was because it was fun. "Sport was more avocation and pastime than career and business."[27] Players still needed to sell themselves to the public as well as to team owners. But as the expanded media coverage increased public interest and revenues, professional sports teams took on more of the properties of large, formal corporations. Players regularly turned to professional agents to represent their interests in the various aspects of their careers. Many players are even corporations unto themselves. Collective bargaining has become regularized, and even strikes have come to be more expected. Player and management confrontations are more prevalent and unions are more dominant. Free agency has given players much more leverage in their push for higher salaries. Professional sports is no longer primarily a game; it is a rational business in which every employee and manager expects a profit:

> The commercial sport industry seeks to organize events on strict market principles—namely the pursuit of capital accumulation—rather than the satisfaction of individual personal and social needs. Although the industry goes to great lengths in advertising and public relations to make the public think it is nurturing play forms and traditional values, it actually has little to do with the human play impulse and traditional conceptions of personal development, family, and community.[28]

The worlds of the professional sports and celebrity often cross, since many prominent players become celebrities. In addition to such figures, however, the world of celebrity includes stars from the mass media, principally movies and television. Like sports figures, many film stars become cultural icons and models. Because of their box-office draw, they can command large revenues from their films. Like sports celebrities, film celebrities have moved from being owned by studios to being free agents who decide to sign or not sign contracts for single pictures. In this situation, as in sports, professional agents become more important as they try to groom, promote, and sell their clients. This drives up the prices of celebrity services, as free agency pushed salary demands up in professional sports.

To a great extent, celebrities are social creations. This is not surprising, given advances in movie-making technology and the rise in the significance of agents, public relations, and media coverage over the last several decades. All of these help manufacture a celebrity. "Beginning in the 1950s, . . . celebrity began to be commonly represented not only as useful to selling and business but as a business itself, created by selling. . . . Terms began to change: the celebrity was becoming 'merchandise,' 'inventory,' 'property,' a 'product,' a 'commodity,' while the fans were becoming 'markets.'"[29]

The interrelationship between fans and the film star is critical in the building and maintaining of celebrity. The fans can see the public persona of the star on screen, but they also want to know something about what he or she is *really* like, in *private* life. A distinction is assumed between their public and private lives, and between their acting image and authentic selves. The interweaving and masterminding of a celebrity's identity for the public is the job of the agent, which means that what is said by the celebrity, to whom it is said, and how it is said become critical in the development of celebrity. The public's access to behind-the-scenes information about celebrities aids in creating a feeling that celebrities have to struggle with problems, needs, and desires like everyone else. In this sense they have an ordinary quality that makes them seem familiar. But their stardom and lifestyle also make them seem distant and different from the rest of us. "The combination of familiarity and extraordinariness gives the celebrity its ideological power."[30] Consider Harrison Ford. On the one hand, he seems as familiar as an old shoe, a family man who does woodworking; on the other hand, he is among the most-in-demand stars in Hollywood. He is at once common and exceptional.

Screen presentations allow celebrities to construct an ideal-typical hero or villain, whose characteristics and actions resonate as examples or antitheses of basic American values. That is, they bring to mind the importance of individualism, honesty, integrity, and other cultural characteristics we admire. This "admiring identification" with celebrities not only makes them seem different or even better than us but it also reinforces celebrities as a "center of cultural capital" in our society. The hope is, of course, that this capital can be turned into economic profit.[31] In addition, celebrity creates political power in that the star's public image incorporates core American values and themes: "It is the capacity of these public figures to embody the collective in the individual, which identifies their cultural signs as powerful."[32] Ultimately, it is their packaging and presentation as a commodity that gives celebrities their psychological, economic, and political power.

As in film, celebrities are also manufactured on the television screen. Similar to movies and images of film stars, television images blur the differences between the real and the unreal, the fake and the authentic. Soap-opera stars and popular TV hosts appear to be regular people just like us, acting out and discussing the kinds of problems that we all face in our everyday lives. In their presentations, there is an emphasis on the familiar.[33] News anchors have also evolved into commodities, becoming part of television's "star system" and representing the cultures of their respective networks. In recent years, they too have become celebrities, giving out less information and more opinion. But they are in the business of attracting audiences and must compete with each other. The result has been a "blurring of boundaries between news and fictional programming—where information increasingly resembles entertainment."[34] In the businesses of both film and television, the objectives are to sell the celebrity product to the consumer for the sake of higher profits, and perhaps to use the cultural capital of celebrities for greater power in cultural and political arenas.

Capitalism in Entertainment

Celebrities in sports and film are commodities being sold in a competitive capitalist market. How valuable they are on the market depends on the effectiveness of the organizational structure that markets them and the ideology they promote. In tracing its development, Marx noted several distinct organizational phases through which capitalism passed. These phases progressed as new technologies for higher efficiency became available to the capitalist, and their introduction into the production process altered the relationship between owners and workers and among the workers themselves. In the first stage of *cooperation,* as Marx dubbed it, free workers were brought together by a capitalist owner under the same roof to produce a product. The greater the number of workers, the greater the production, and therefore the greater the profit. In trying to improve efficiency and the bottom line, capitalists next perfected *job specialization* to take advantages of the best talents of each individual and to eliminate waste. Each person had a specialized task, which, when put together with the narrow tasks of others, combined to create an efficient organization whose synchronized production process could increase profit. The drive for even greater profit then pushed capitalism into its third, or *machine,* stage in which capitalists removed the heavy cost of labor by replacing living labor with machines (dead labor). In Marx's logic, this eventually exacerbated the unemployment problem and further set into motion a series of systemic problems (e.g., overproduction, monopolization, class consciousness), which eventually led to capitalism's collapse.

There are some parallels between these stages as proposed by Marx and the shifts that have occurred in the marketing of celebrities. As in any significant shift, the material historical conditions must be right before changes can occur. Similar to Marx's *first phase,* sport and film celebrities were brought under the roofs of one team or studio and were required to do whatever the owner asked.[35] They were essentially owned by that firm. The more actors a studio had, for example, the more it could produce and the greater its profits. But as media technologies changed both within and outside film production, the power of studios was shaken and undermined. Within the film industry, the development of new techniques such as the close-up created a foundation for the full production of celebrities or stars. Outside the industry, and perhaps most prominently, the rise of television introduced a serious competitor that endangered the profits of movie studios. In other words, a shift in the material conditions of technology and the consequent weakening of the power of studios helped lay the groundwork for a new set of relationships between actors and studio owners. In Marx's language, the existing relationships became "fetters," or binding chains, on the improvements that were occurring in technologies. "At a certain state of their development, the material forces of production in society come in conflict with the existing relations of production. . . . From forms of development of the forces of production these relations turn into their fetters."[36]

Political pressures from the court and/or employees also helped speed changes in these relationships. For example, in the 1948 Supreme Court case of *United States v. Paramount Pictures, Inc. et al.,* the court effectively broke down some of the monopolistic practices of the studio in the production and distribution of films. Into the breach left by these developments stepped the *second phase*—new independent studios, which created greater competition. Also stepping in as a formidable new force were talent agents and a whole series of new specialized positions to represent and promote stars in their careers. Improvements in the techniques of audience research and marketing strategies eased the selling of celebrities to the public. As an organization of specialized interdependent parts, the publicity machine of celebrities makes their careers more profitable. Celebrity specialization also occurs as some actors are typecast or stereotyped as appropriate for certain kinds of roles. Unlike the classic *third phase* of capitalism, it is improbable that this product can be replaced by a machine. The best that might be done to maximize profit is to use the image of the celebrity as a mass-produced object as much as possible. In this case, the image replaces the real person, just as the machine replaces the worker.

The vast and accelerating improvements in media technology make it easier to sell a celebrity product to the consuming public. Image making has become much more sophisticated. The greater sensitivity by the celebrity's army of agents and assistants to nuanced images of stars projected to the audience has deepened the ways in which celebrity power can reach into and manipulate the public. This creates a greater possibility for ideological control. There is some concern about this power and pervasiveness of such control in our democracy: "Entertainment celebrity is an imperialist phenomenon, moving into new arenas and making them over in its own image."[37] The smoothness of the advanced technologies make the processes by which celebrities are created and their images maintained more difficult to discern. In effect, the process becomes mystified by the sophistication of the technology, and the actual mechanisms of manipulation become less and less clear.

Enchantment and Disenchantment of Celebrity

As I have mentioned in an earlier discussion, Weber imagined the modern world as one in which the quality of enchantment was rapidly disappearing with the onslaught of the powerful rational forces of science, technology, capitalism, and bureaucracy. The meaning of *rational* in Weber's work is decidedly multidimensional, and can be associated with terms such as *deliberate, systematic, calculable, impersonal, instrumental, exact, quantitative, rule governed, predictable, methodical, purposeful, sober, scrupulous, efficacious, intelligible,* and *consistent.* In every major institutional area, "rationalization has involved the depersonalization of social relationships, the refinement of techniques of calculation, the enhancement of the social importance of specialized knowledge, and the extension of technically rational control over both natural and social processes."[38]

The world of the irrational and enchanted—magic, the supernatural, and the emotional—was largely doomed in Weber's vision of modern society. Society was becoming rational and *dis*-enchanted. In a general sense, then, the rational and irrational elements of social life are basically incompatible. The irrational force of charisma, for example, does not mix well with formalism and the fixity of bureaucracy. Yet in contemporary celebrities, we see a commingling of the irrational and the rational side by side, the efficient creation and selling of charismatic personalities through the use of formal publicity organizations. The basis of celebrities' attraction is largely emotional and irrational, yet the image on which this emotion is based is managed by a rational, profit-oriented organization made up of a variety of specialists. This has led David Marshall to suggest that the changes that would be required in Weber's analysis "may be too radical to fit into the original Weberian model."[39]

The heavy-duty stars in sports and the media that we have come to love possess what Max Weber called *charisma*. By that, he meant "a certain quality of an individual personality by virtue of which he is considered extraordinary and treated as endowed with supernatural, superhuman, or at least specifically exceptional powers or qualities."[40] This quality is the basis of the legitimate authority that the person in question possesses, and it is because of this that charisma must be sustained if the sway of the person over others is to continue. The celebrity's agent and technology are critical in maintaining charisma because it depends on the willingness of the audience to grant such authority. Without such a free giving, the quality of charisma disappears. Through the ministrations of agents, the audience is changed and brought into the adoring fold from "within." It is the audience's thinking and feeling that are revolutionized to make them followers. Like tradition, charisma is founded "on a sense of loyalty and obligation which always has a religious aura."[41]

In addition to its dependence on a submissive audience, another of the significant properties of charisma in the case of its application to celebrities is that, unlike authority based on formal position in an organization, there is no delimited area of power. It can be expanded into different spheres. This is one reason why some critics worry about the democratic implications of celebrity (as noted earlier). It allows broad-based control. Ronald Reagan can become president, Paul Newman can sell his spaghetti sauce, and Charlton Heston can become president of the National Rifle Association largely because of their charismatic-celebrity status. Celebrities become authorities on everything.

The subjective quality of charisma makes it inherently unstable, however. One has only to think of the celebrities who come and go as their legitimacy is lost, enjoying the spotlight for only 15 minutes. Sometimes charismatic authority can be sustained for a long period of time. This requires the "routinization" of charisma or its transfer to a more permanent form of organization. In the world of celebrity, for example, the personalities of deceased stars can continue on through the clubs and other organizations created to represent them. James Dean, Marilyn Monroe, and Elvis Presley all live on through these organizations. When this happens, charisma has been depersonalized and "attached to the incumbent of an office or to an institutional structure regardless of the persons involved."[42]

In the case of celebrities, their persona is in the hands of a large number of employees whose job it is to protect and promote their charismatic hold over their followers. The human, technological, and organizational machinery that work behind the scenes in this manner constitute a rational structure. In effect, this structure works for many celebrities; in this sense, it is impersonal like a bureaucracy. To accomplish its objective, this organization ideally contains career-oriented individuals hired on the basis of their ability. This is one way in which it infuses efficiency or low cost into its operation. Ironically, while Weber emphasized the removal of all personal elements in bureaucracies for the sake of efficient operation, the presence of personal connections and friendships may enhance the effectiveness of organizations whose goal is publicity for their clients. The very nature of their objectives, the successful packaging of personalities, would seem to make an element of the irrational inevitable in such organizations. The so-called packaging of personalities suggests that successful celebrity organizations rationalize the irrational: "It has effectively integrated the concept of personality differences and individuality into a system of exchange; and . . . it has worked toward the rationalization of the audience to see these representations of personality in the celebrity as legitimate forms of identification and cultural value."[43]

An implicit danger lies in the use of a rational organization to create or impose cultural values. Values cannot be derived from the rational process found in these organizations; nor can they be derived from facts or empirical study in general. The danger in the mix of rationality and cultural values in celebrity organizations consists of the fact that effectively marketed celebrities can unduly influence the values of individuals in their audience, often without their knowing it. This influence undermines what should be the free basis of value selection on the part of the individual. In Weber's view, decisions are "the task of the acting, willing person: he weighs and chooses from among the values involved according to his own conscience and his personal view of the world. . . . The act of choice itself is his own responsibility."[44] It seems to me that, as Weber indicates, since the most important problems involved in making social policies are not technical but rather normative, the inordinate influence of powerful celebrities unduly restricts the act of free choice necessary in the individual formulation of personal values. Here again, democracy and the power of celebrity clash.

Celebrities use the cult of personality to unduly influence their audience. Paradoxically, the very effectiveness of their rational publicity machines reintroduces an element of enchantment into the world because they manufacture an air of mystery and magic about stars. This is done by carefully cultivating both an aloofness and a sense of familiarity with celebrities. The force of their charismatic personalities also perpetuates the irrational, the enchantment of modern life. But it must be remembered that celebrities become a source of enchantment only because they have been effectively marketed as commodities by disenchanted, rational publicity organizations.

THE VALUE OF HUMAN LIFE

Weber was very clear in his view that the rational institutions of modern life cannot provide us with a set of ultimate values by which to organize our lives. **Value-rational action** is behavior in which the most effective means obtainable are used to reach a goal that is determined by a fundamental set of values in which the individual believes. The more *absolute* the values and the more *resolutely* individuals wish to enact them, "the more 'irrational' in this sense the action is. . . . For the more unconditionally the actor devotes himself to this value for its own sake . . . the less is he influenced by considerations of the consequences of his action."[45] Such values are not to be created by celebrities, but only by freely acting individuals. Values are critical because they give direction and meaning to life; they provide life with its worth. For Weber, the dominance of formal over substantive rationality in modern life provides a justification for viewing human beings as commodities, as means to ends. Human life as a value in itself becomes less important.

Since the early 1980s, there have been some serious attempts to determine the value of human life, and inevitably these have always meant trying to place a price tag on an individual's head.[46] In other words, *value* has been defined economically rather than socially, religiously, and so forth. As Simmel suggested, money becomes a univeral standard in which qualitative differences between objects are erased. This requires putting a dollar value on the lives of individuals. Many of these assessments of human life were instigated by changes in governmental regulations in 1981, which required that any proposed new regulation that could cost an industry more than $100 million would have to demonstrate, in detail, how the economic benefits of the regulation would outweigh its costs. Increased awareness of the human effects of pollution and the rising costs of health care, most notably extraordinary measures to keep individuals alive, have also spurred attempts to arrive at a value for human life. Although the attempts to place a price tag on human life are repugnant to many, to others they seem essential since we live in a society that has limited resources.

These efforts have produced some interesting price-tag formulas. One of these asked respondents how much their lives are worth to them. Essentially, respondents were asked what salary they would need to accept a job with clearly defined risks. If, for example, the job is known to kill 1 out of every 1,000 workers, and workers are willing to accept the job for $5,000 more than the average safe job, then the value they have placed on their lives is $5,000 × 1,000, or $5,000,000. Other attempts have relied on individuals' actual behavior to assess the value they place on their lives. For example, another analyst estimated the value of human life by finding out how much more people were willing to pay for a house in an area with little pollution.

The value placed on human life also appears to depend on the social status and culture of the people involved. "A cost-benefits analysis will always wind up favoring the more prosperous or socially well-off," argues Arthur Caplan, who analyzes ethical issues in medicine.[47] The 1984 Union Carbide chemical disaster in Bhopal required the company to pay $470 million for the 3,300 killed and many more injured. That amounted to only a few thousand dollars per family. Had the accident occurred in the United States, that amount would almost assuredly have been unacceptable. Even within the United States, the value placed on human life appears to depend on the social status of the victims involved. Victims of lower status receive much less attention from authorities and the media than tragedies involving higher-status individuals. The case of JonBenet Ramsey, for example, has taxed many more resources and received much more press than similar cases of unknown child victims. In Los Angeles, the inadvertent killing of a young professional in fashionable Westwood resulted in massive press coverage and increased police patrols. On the other side of town in South Central Los Angeles, and at about the same time, a poor, 67-year-old, wheelchair-bound woman was shot in a drive-by shooting. Yet her death got little attention from the media and police officials.[48]

The value of human life has become rationalized and trivialized in a variety of ways today. Putting a price tag on people is only one way in which market values have infiltrated the most sacred elements of society. The remolding of the human body through cosmetic surgery and the marketing of sport and media celebrities are both illustrations of the contemporary commodification of human beings. In the following section, I wish to discuss briefly further events in medicine as an area that exemplifies the rationalization and trivialization of human life.

Rational Medicine and the Giving of Life

Health-care professionals deal with disease, pain, suffering, and death on a daily basis. The constant onslaught of such experiences can have a devastating effect if internalized and taken personally. To remain involved and be effective, physicians and nurses need to be somewhat detached in their approach to such difficulties. In medical school, students are taught to develop a "detached concern" for their patients, an attitude that precariously balances aloofness and intimacy.[49] To remain effective and consistent, nurses learn to "routinize" the disasters that surround them as a way of psychologically distancing themselves from the wrenching problems of patients. Learning one's way around the hospital, knowing the jargon and the techniques required in detail, and learning to recognize the various patient types, are the principal means by which nurses get into a routine manner of acting toward the tragedies they confront. When they have been so routinized, "the outsider's sense of dread, or dismay, at what is happening with patients has vanished; the mention of serious disease or death gets a nod, perhaps, but no more. Here in the hospital, to these nurses, terrible things have become ordinary."[50]

Rationalization in medicine is also reflected in the professional attitude taken toward the human body. In medical school, students engage in cadaver stories and black humor about body parts as a way of socializing themselves into controlling their emotions. These are methods of training physicians on how to deal with their feelings when faced with disease and death. Cadaver stories would likely be considered by outsiders to be gross and in poor taste, but for medical students, they constitute a rite of passage into the cool and professional world of medicine. Students who react too emotionally to these episodes are in trouble:

> Behaviors that indicate the presence of anxiety, fear, and revulsion are character-
> ized in these stories as both inappropriate and sanctionable. Conversely, behaviors
> reflecting humor and "good-natured" camaraderie are characterized as both appro-
> priate and functional. Cadaver stories stress that within medicine, *the cadaver
> should exist as a learning tool and an object for manipulation rather than as a for-
> merly living human being.*[51]

The progressive commodification of the body is also found in the market-ing and use of body parts. In 1991, over 400 blood centers in the United States collected and marketed blood products, and 95 percent of those who gave blood were paid for it. Sperm and eggs are also body parts for sale. About 172,000 women receive artificial insemination each year, with the average sperm donor receiving about $50 for each donation. More than 65 U.S. medical clinics also have donor egg programs for women who are infertile. Finally, even surrogate wombs are available for women who will not or cannot carry their own chil-dren.[52]

Obviously, these transactions raise serious ethical and economic issues. Perhaps most controversial is the real prospect of human cloning, recently raised by University of Chicago scientist Richard Seed, who says that he has the ability to carry it out today. Human cloning may represent the ultimate intrusion of ratio-nal science into human life. Although numerous medical benefits are likely to be reaped from human cloning, there are also moral and spiritual questions about it.[53]

Rationalization in medicine, as in many other areas, has both positive and negative consequences. On the one hand, it makes professionals more effective and in many cases promotes human health; on the other hand, because it depersonalizes and commodifies the human body, it appears to cheapen and weaken the value of human beings. The dilemma of balancing humane, quality care to patients with the maintenance of low costs and profits is at the heart of problems faced by both not-for-profit and for-profit health-care plans. Too often the concern for profits and the drive to remain economically competitive override the priority of quality care. Although 80 percent of employers list cost as the most important criterion when they choose a health plan for their employees, the public in general believes they have a right to decent health care and that cost should be less important: "Although the U.S. has currently opted for a market-based health care system, the public has shown by the recurrent eruptions of outrage that it views health care as a social good, and even a right, not a commodity."[54] The clash between the goals of efficiency and practicality and the goal of honoring the sacredness of people is likely to intensify as science and economic/market considerations become more intimately involved in our lives.

CONCLUSION

The treatment of human life by celebrity and medical professionals is certainly different, but it also betrays certain similarities. Both groups treat human beings as commodities, and as Marx suggested, in capitalist society everything tends to become a commodity, including people. The aloofness of professionals from their audiences and patients suggest a social distancing between people that classical theorists viewed as a characteristic of modern society.

In the case of health care, there is often a priority and even an obsession given to the bottom line at the expense of adequate care. Simmel would not be surprised. With respect to the contemporary dominance of money in our thinking, Simmel observed that "never has an object . . . so thoroughly and unreservedly developed into a psychological absolute value, into a completely engrossing final purpose governing our practical consciousness."[55] This does not mean that people become intentionally mean-spirited, but that money and rationality encourage them to become mentally distant from others. "Certainly there is something callous about the purely rationalistic treatment of people and things. Yet this is not a positive impulse but simply results from pure logic being unaffected by respect, kindness and delicacies of feeling."[56] Money becomes the standard measure by which to evaluate objects, humans, and services. Money's value continues to increase as the range of things defined and measured in terms of it grows. Under those conditions, it becomes an end or value in itself. Money is "the outstanding and most perfect example of the psychological raising of means to ends."[57]

Adding to the impersonality and rationality of attitude promoted by money is the dominance of the mind over the heart. In modern society, Simmel viewed the city especially as the place where intellect rules over the heart. The blasé attitude that urbanites develop deindividualizes and desubjectivizes others so that they can deal with people as categories without taking them to heart. This promotes at least a superficial callousness toward others. "The blasé person . . . has completely lost the feeling for value differences. He experiences all things as being of an equally dull and grey hue, as not worth getting excited about."[58] In Simmel's view, there is a strong consistency between processes of rationalization, intellectualization, calculability, a money economy, urbanization, and attitudes toward other people.

Rationalization as a central force in modern society was emphasized by all the classical theorists, and most recognized its mixed consequences. Durkheim saw science becoming an influential institution in modern society. The disenchantment caused by the increasing influence of science, often at the expense of religion, has encouraged a more intellectualized, nonsacred perspective on human beings. The occupational specialization that he predicted is demonstrated in the existence of narrow professionals in the medical field who operate on different parts of the body. In Marx's view, however, such specialization would encourage a feeling of alienation from the whole patient. In recent years, there has been an increased emphasis on family practice and holistic medicine as an antidote to excessive specialization. Some of Weber's interpreters as well have associated the rationalization and disenchantment of modern society with increased callousness. The concern for numbers, precision, and calculation outweigh the value of human life. Bureaucratic efficiency has made it possible to think of people as cyphers rather than as individuals. The principal ideas used from each theorist in understanding the issues explored in this chapter are listed in Comparative Chart 6.1.

In this chapter, I have stressed the general theme of social distance—between our selves and our bodies, between celebrities and audiences, and between medical professionals and patients. Indeed, social distance has been a recurring emphasis in most of the chapters up to this point. In Chapter 7, I turn to the polarization of economic resources as a final instance of social distancing and as a possible source of disunity.

COMPARATIVE CHART 6.1   Basic Ideas from Each Theorist Used in Analyses of Chapter Issues

	Body as Commodity	Celebrity as Commodity	Value of Human Life
Marx	Class structure affecting access to surgery and beauty standards; body parts as fetishes and commodities; exchange value of body parts and the profit motive in maintaining the beauty ideology emotional labor	Stages of capitalism as paralleling phases of film industry; ideological control through technology	Value of life determined by economic standing
Durkheim	Distinction between sacred and profane; the merging of body with the sacred—models as totems and representations of a collective ideal anorexia as an attempt to leave profane and enter the sacred		
Simmel			Money as the basis for determining value of human life in modern society; urban life; blasé attitude, and callousness
Weber		Rationalization and disenchantment as characteristics of modern society; charismatic authority of celebrities; routinization of charisma in dead celebrities; use of rational bureaucracy to sell the irrational	Value-rationality and the importance of substantive rationality in society; need for impersonality and rational-ization in medical care

QUESTIONS TO PONDER

1. In what way can it be argued that an overemphasis on one's physical appearance alienates individuals from themselves? Is the body *part* of the self or *separate* from the self? Explain your answer.

2. Several of the classical theorists believed that much of modern life has become objectified and rationalized. In addition to the areas of the body, celebrity, and medicine, in what other areas has modern life become objectified and rationalized?

3. Is it possible to effectively unite the rational and irrational, mental and emotional dimensions of life to create a more humane society? Why or why not? Should social theorists even be concerned about such an issue? Explain your answer.

CHAPTER 7

THE POLARIZATION
OF ECONOMIC RESOURCES

CHAPTER IN BRIEF

- **INTRODUCTION**

economic inequality and issues of separation and social distance; presence of multidimensional economic inequality

- **INSIDE THE U.S. CLASS STRUCTURE**

Marxian conception of class and class structure; Wright's view of U.S. class structure; trends in earnings and benefits; distribution of income and decline of middle class; wealth inequality and its broader significance; growth of corporate concentration; economic events and economic inequality

- **UNDERSTANDING PROCESSES OF ECONOMIC INEQUALITY**

economic and relational nature of class; stages of capitalism and recent economic trends; alienation in work; growth of proletariat under capitalism; inadequacies and strengths of Marx's class theory (Marx); labor class and capitalists as social circles; capitalists as unified by use of money as form of exchange; power of money; opposition of employee and

employer classes; social circles in classes as sources of cohesion and individuality (Simmel)

- **ECONOMIC INEQUALITY BETWEEN STATUS GROUPS**

income, wealth, and earnings inequality among racial and ethnic groups; broad forces behind economic inequality between groups; income, wealth, earnings, and gender

- **ACCOUNTING FOR INEQUALITY BETWEEN GROUPS**

race and sex as bases of status groups; the perceived biological bases of racial inequality, its justification, and maintenance of status boundaries; ideology and continuation of inequality through historical monopolization of resources (Weber); gradual disappearance of race and gender as bases for position; abnormal forms of division of labor and continuance of racial and gender inequality; justice as a modern task (Durkheim)

INTRODUCTION

Economic inequality is a fitting topic for this final chapter because it is related to so many of the other kinds of social distance and separation discussed so far. It is one condition that has set off individuals and groups from each other, and it has more often served as a centrifugal than a centripetal force in the United States. Such inequality is implicated in the issues of egoism and obligations to community, gated communities and segregation, political corruption and cynicism, and the ability to pay for cosmetic surgery.

There is abundant evidence for the continuity and recent increase in economic inequality in the United States. Information on social classes, earnings, incomes, poverty, and wealth all point to continued and significant economic discrepancies between individuals and groups. Obviously, economic inequality itself has a variety of dimensions and, because of the everyday importance of money, attempts to measure economic inequality have been surrounded by controversy. In the first section of this chapter, I will discuss the nature of the U.S. class structure and the earnings and wealth distributions within it. Following that discussion will be applications of Marx and Simmel to these aspects of economic inequality. In the second section, I will present data on the occupational, income, and earning differences between the races and sexes, and then interpret these differences using ideas from Durkheim and Weber.

INSIDE THE U.S. CLASS STRUCTURE

Social class is a very controversial concept in social science. Much of the controversy about the importance of social class revolves on the meaning and definition that has been given to it. Rather than launch into a detailed discussion of the varieties of definitions of social class, I will concentrate here on the Marxian conceptualization.

Marx contended that the class structure of a society and a person's position within it were directly tied to the nature of the economy within which they were embedded. A capitalist economy such as that in the United States is defined primarily by its emphasis on private ownership of the means of production. Those who own and have control over the physical means (property) and social means (labor power) of production are in one class, whereas those who own little and have little control are in another. Over the last two decades, Erik Wright has attempted to outline what the U.S. class structure looks like from a Marxian perspective.[1] His most recent depictions define class position in terms of different bases of exploitation. One can exploit or be exploited because of position with respect to (1) property, (2) organizational authority, and/or (3) expertise. Where one falls on these criteria defines one's class position.

Using these criteria, Wright describes three broad classes in the U.S. economy. He concludes that only about 15 percent of those in the economic system are in the group of owners. Within this ownership group are those who have employees and others who are self-employed without employees. It is primarily the fraction of large employers in this group who are generally considered to be the capitalist class. Among the nonowners, there are those who have organizational authority and/or expertise, such as managers and professionals, and who make up a kind of second or middle class. They are in a "contradictory location," according to Wright, because although they owe allegiance to owners and act on their behalf, they are also employees, and thus share some characteristics with other workers. This middle group makes up approximately 45 percent of the labor force. Finally, the third group is the working class, which includes about 40 percent of those in the economy. They are defined by the fact that they are nonowners, nonexperts, and nonmanagers. Consequently, they are in a position of being exploited by the property, organizational authority, and expertise of others. With respect to the two polar classes (i.e., the capitalist and working classes), most models of the U.S. class structure suggest that the capitalist class makes up 1 to 2 percent and the working class makes up to 40 to 50 percent of the population.

These classes are clearly distinguished by their earnings, income, and wealth. Most research on earnings differences has uncovered high earnings inequality among workers, and some suggest the discrepancies grew between the 1970s and mid-1990s.[2] Between the late 1980s and mid-1990s, hourly wages dropped for the bottom 80 percent while they rose among high-wage workers. While the wages of most workers suffered, chief executive officers (CEOs) have done quite well. In 1995, the average CEO's pay was 141 times that of the average factory worker. That same year, the average total compensation package for CEOs was $3,746,392.[3]

There appears to be a connection between the high compensation of CEOs and the layoffs experienced by many workers. Studies indicate that in 1996, CEO pay at the companies with the highest number of layoffs rose higher than average. "Wall Street rewards CEOs for making layoffs by pushing up stock prices, which are the basis for the biggest component of CEO compensation stock options."[4] When the value of fringe benefits is added for consideration, the economic gap between high- and low-ranking workers appears even greater, since it has been primarily workers at the bottom of the scale who have been most likely to lose access to benefits. In 1996, only 26 percent of workers in the bottom 10 percent had health insurance provided by their employers, compared to 84 percent of those in the middle and 90 percent of those in the top 10 percent. Similar discrepancies exist on pension plans and paid vacations.[5] Benefits and earnings inequality is especially evident in urban areas where racial segregation and large gaps between the rich and the poor go together. Some of the same forces (e.g., changes in job distributions) are involved in maintaining both ghettos and earnings inequality.

Class or position within the economic structure directly affects income. Earnings from employment, however, is only one source of income. Individuals can receive money from a variety of other sources, including family and the government. Like that of earnings, the distribution of income from all sources in the United States is highly unequal. In 1976, the bottom fifth of households in the United States possessed 4.4 percent of all income, whereas the top fifth owned 43.3 percent. By 1996, that difference had changed to 3.7 percent and 49.0 percent, respectively. By this standard, the rich got richer and the poor got poorer. In 1996, the average incomes of individuals in the top 20 percent of households was over 13 times that of households in the bottom 20 percent, compared to 11 times as great in 1967. In part, this reflects an increase in the rate of income growth among the top 20 percent that was well over twice as fast as that in the bottom 20 percent.[6] Also during this period, the percentages of individuals in middle-income categories ($25,000–$75,000) declined.

The breaking up and splitting of the middle-income class may be polarizing those within it who are well educated, professional, and mobile, from those who are less educated, stuck in dead-end jobs, and less adaptable to change. Partly, this is related to the increased demand for workers in the service economy at both the high and low ends of the occupational scale. This has bred some class hostility between these sectors of the middle class. While the young white professionals with their chic values and up-to-date expertise adapt to economic changes and prosper, embittered less-educated workers feel they are being left behind and forgotten. Sidney Tracy, a lab technician who lost his job, symbolizes the feelings of those in the lower sector: "The working man, he ain't got a chance." "Everything [Democratic liberals] do, everything they want to do, is against us," replies Carl Biggs, an unemployed telephone technician.[7]

Wealth is even more unequally distributed than income. *Wealth* refers to the value of all of one's assets minus one's debts. Because it includes most everything owned that is of economic value (e.g., businesses, investments, homes, cars, etc.), wealth is a more complete measure of the economic status of an individual than is income.

Moreover, wealth provides its owner with a variety of economic opportunities and tools not possessed by the nonwealthy. It permits the creation of gated communities and other exclusive residential areas. Consider the housing situation in Jackson Hole, Wyoming, for example. Nested among the Teton Mountains and the Snake River, and near two national parks, the natural beauty of Jackson Hole is breathtaking. Unfortunately, only a few can afford to take advantage of the vista on a permanent basis. In 1994, the average cost of a home in Jackson Hole was $561,000, not affordable for the average workers who serve those wealthy who come to live here. Like the exclusive gated communities discussed in Chapter 4, Jackson Hole is a "golden ghetto" that "sets up sharp class conflicts, with new residents pushing for bans on trailer parks because they mar the view." [8] The influence of wealth in local and national policy-making was demonstrated earlier in discussions of zoning and campaign contributions. This power of wealth also feeds the political cynicism noted in Chapter 5. Finally, the power of wealth also extends beyond its sheer amount. For example, significant stock ownership in a company that has connections with another corporation may give the owner indirect influence over the latter organization, as well. Current wealth can also be used to create more wealth, which can be passed on to future generations within the same families.

The significance of wealth for creating opportunities and control over one's life is apparent. Expensive and repeated cosmetic plastic surgery, for example, can be indulged in only by those who can afford it. Important as wealth is, however, current information on its distribution is not as available as data on income. Figures from the early 1990s are available, however. In 1993, those with incomes in the top 20 percent had a median wealth or net worth of $118,006, compared to $4,249 for those in the bottom 20 percent. Wealth concentration increased from the late 1970s into the early 1990s. In 1993, the bottom 20 percent owned only 7 percent of all the net wealth in the United States, and the top 20 percent possessed 44 percent of it. An extraordinary 99 percent of the gains that were had in the 1980s went to the top 20 percent, and the richest 1 percent received 62 percent. This means that only *1 percent* of the gains in wealth went to the bottom *80 percent*.[9] Not surprisingly, this is tied to the fact that the types of assets held by the wealthy differ from those of others. The wealthy are more likely to have significant amounts of stock and related investments, which would allow them to benefit handsomely from gains in the financial market.

The growing inequality in income and wealth is paralleled by increasing concentration in the economy in general. In 1950, the largest 100 industrial corporations in the United States controlled just under 40 percent of all industrial assets. By 1992, that figure had risen to almost 75 percent. Additionally, one must consider that many of these corporations have worldwide markets in which concentration is also increasing. In the United States, even greater degrees of concentration exist in the fields of communication, utilities, insurance, and finance than in industry. These continued concentrations result in part from mergers in the 1990s among significant players in the economy. "In brief, the central feature of the American and world economy is the concentration of resources in relatively few large corporations.... It is clear that society is not going to return to a small, romanticized, perhaps mythical, world of individual enterprise."[10] The concentration of corporate and individual wealth are connected because of the significant amount of stock held by the wealthy in blue-chip corporations. In other words, the wealth of the richest is closely tied to core institutions in the economy. Arguably, the power of the wealthy and their ties to international corporations provide an independence to these individuals that makes their obligations to others and their communities less compelling for them. If they are independently wealthy, why should they feel obligations to anyone? Similarly, why should those on the bottom who feel left out or discriminated against feel a sense of commitment to others?

The fact that the distribution of economic resources is implicated in issues surrounding individual/community obligations, residential segregation, feelings of cynicism, and medical opportunities makes its understanding especially important. A variety of reasons have been offered to account for the increase in economic inequality in recent decades. Among these are changes in the occupational structure and the demand for certain kinds of jobs. Demand for workers in manufacturing jobs has declined, while that for service and professional workers has increased. Service and professional positions contain wider variations in salaries and wages, thus prompting more inequality in earnings. Downsizing, restructuring, and a greater emphasis on efficiency has created layoffs in permanent positions and increases in temporary positions with few fringe benefits attached. Recent declines in unionization, coupled with governmental tax reform that cuts rates for the wealthy as well as cuts programs for the needy, have also been thought partly responsible for growing economic inequality.[11]

To make sense of all these conditions and reactions requires an understanding of the forces driving the changes occurring in the occupational, wealth, and income structures. The reasons discussed here pinpoint specific events that foster inequality, but they need to be incorporated into a broader historical and structural perspective for their meaning to be fully realized. The classical theorists help provide that framework.

UNDERSTANDING PROCESSES OF ECONOMIC INEQUALITY

Modern theories of class inequality owe much to Karl Marx's analysis of capitalism and the class structure within it. Even though, as some critics have said, a proletarian revolution has not happened in the most advanced capitalist nation, Marx identified certain core features and processes within capitalism that have shaped its development. In other words, if one takes a broad instead of a rigid purist view of Marx's method and theory, it is possible to use them as effective tools for understanding what is going on with respect to economic inequality. What occurs in the economy heavily influences shifts in the class structure of any country, including the United States.

As noted earlier, Marx believed that the principal criterion of class position was private property. One's relationship to property and the types of property distinguish the major classes. Thus, for Marx, workers, capitalists, and landowners "form the three great classes of modern society based on the capitalist mode of production."[12] The property and power relationships among individuals in the economy constitute the social relations of production. In other words, property and power tie individuals and groups together within the capitalist system. The property owner depends on workers to produce products, and the worker depends on the owner to provide employment. The relational nature of class position is important to understand because, in Marx's view, it is the basis on which one class exploits another and enhances its position while the position of the other declines. To see how the relationships between classes change over time, it is first necessary to understand changes that occur in the capitalist system as it develops.

I will not review in detail the specific stages through which capitalism passes according to Marx, but will say only that the development of successive stages is motivated by the drive for greater and greater profit on the part of capitalists, and depends, minimally, on advances in technology. Here is where Marx's observations can shed light on the downsizing, push for efficiency, layoffs, and other changes currently happening in the U.S. economy.

To be profitable, corporations must successfully compete in the marketplace. In the early stage of capitalism, this meant hiring more workers and bringing them under one roof to produce more products than their competitors. Owners were heavily dependent on workers to do the "productive" (manual) labor that was necessary. This produced profits, but as technology advanced and new methods were discovered around the turn of the twentieth century, capitalists were able to better organize the work of employees to increase efficiency and ultimately profits. The detailed division of labor (i.e., specialization) allowed owners to utilize only those narrow abilities of a worker in which he or she excelled. By doing this, each laborer carried out a small narrow task and basically became part of a huge human machine that manufactured goods in the most efficient manner: "The one-sidedness and the deficiencies of the detail laborer become perfections when he is a part of the collective laborer. The habit of doing only one thing converts him into a never failing instrument, while his connection with the whole mechanism compels him to work with the regularity of the parts of a machine."[13]

Obviously, Marx was not as sanguine about the division of labor in modern society as, for example, Durkheim was. In the capitalist stage of manufacture, as Marx called it, the ordinary laborer is changed "into a crippled monstrosity, by forcing his detail dexterity at the expense of a world of productive capabilities and instincts." The worker becomes "a mere fragment of his own body" over which he or she has little control.[14] Under these conditions, Marx argued, alienation of workers from their work, their products, others, and themselves intensifies. The division of labor benefits the capitalist owner of business, who sees production rise, at the same time that it demeans and degrades the individual worker. Capitalists advance at the direct expense of workers, meaning that capitalists are in their lofty position *because* they exploit employees. Class is based on a social and exploitative relationship.

The alienating effects of detailed unchanging labor have been demonstrated in many studies over the last several decades. Research conducted on job satisfaction and alienation among employees has repeatedly confirmed that, in general, those in a highly coordinated detailed division who carry out routine, repetitive, narrow tasks that they do not define or structure are more likely to be dissatisfied than other employees.[15] This does not appear to have changed much since the 1950s, when the early studies were done. Ruth Milkman recently finished an on-site study of the General Motors automobile assembly plant in Linden, New Jersey, and her results echo those of past research: "In the wake of the economic upheavals of the 1980s and 1990s, the classic questions of worker alienation and degradation have been virtually obliterated from public memory. Yet for workers at places like GM-Linden, the daily humiliations of the assembly line continue to rankle."[16]

The "daily humiliations" of which Milkman speaks continue because that kind of structure is profitable. If it were not profitable, it would be changed. The profit motive informs all major organizational developments, from changes in task design to the creation of new products, to hirings and layoffs, to plant closure and relocation. This means that massive layoffs, moving plants to the South or abroad in search of cheaper labor, and greater use of temporary workers are all merely attempts to keep the business profitable even if it is at the expense of workers. When the Singer Company closed its doors in Elizabeth, New Jersey, the workers felt they had been used: "The company made their money in this area and they became a worldwide financial power through the work of the people in Union County, New Jersey. And then they let them down like a bunch of garbage.... They used the community.... There's such a thing as takers and there's such a thing as givers. [Singer's] were the takers."[17]

Capitalism uses a variety of techniques to maintain and increase its profit. In addition to the division of labor and plant closings caused by the inability of some organizations to compete successfully, Marx cited the introduction of machines displacing workers as a more advanced attempt to keep industry afloat through the reduction of labor costs. As it advances even further, capitalism will eventually spread beyond national boundaries, seeking out new markets for new profits to dominate the world economy.

What must be understood here is that Marx views capitalism as operating according to its own internal laws and logic. The evolution of capitalism is dialectical in nature in that its own structure and changes in that structure bring about oppositional forces that ultimately lead to its demise. The process follows a particular order. Capitalists compete for laborers, bring them together, create an alienating division of labor, then replace the workers with machines, throwing many into unemployment and further misery. Overproduction crises occur because few can now afford to buy the products produced by the increasingly efficient manufacturing process. Some companies go bankrupt, or are bought out by larger ones. Eventually, monopoly capitalism develops in which a few big companies dominate industry. Capital internationalizes, drawing people from around the world into its system.

All of this occurs on capital's side of the process. But in making all these changes to improve profit margins, capitalists have inadvertently created a larger and larger solidified working class that has been progressively emiserated and oppressed. The same process produces internally opposed groups:

> Along with the constantly diminishing number of the magnates of capital, who usurp and monopolize all advantages of this process of transformation, grows the mass of misery, oppression, slavery, degradation, exploitation; but with this too grows the revolt of the working-class, a class always increasing in numbers and disciplined, united, organized by the very mechanism of the process of capitalist production itself.[18]

In the process of capitalist development, workers are only a potential social class—a class-in-itself. It is only under the conditions previously outlined in the evolution of a capitalist economy that they become a class-conscious group—a class-for-itself.

In taking this argument about capitalism's development and applying it to the facts of economic inequality enumerated earlier, we find that, indeed, since early in the twentieth century there has been an increasing centralization of large employers in the United States. Many new companies have gone bankrupt, and a few have been bought up by the workers themselves. There has also been growing income, wealth, and earnings inequality between the top and the bottom. Historically, many workers have engaged in bitter—sometimes violent—battles and strikes with industry and organized into unions to protect their interests. These actions constitute a "class struggle American style."[19]

Despite these occurrences, I think it can be fairly said that Marx underestimated the ability of capitalism to adapt to its own developments, and of the power of the state to quell collective unrest and create a more acquiescent public. Nor has emiseration reached the heights envisioned by Marx, even though inequality has advanced. Finally, the international solidarity of workers that Marx foresaw is nowhere near completion, as unions themselves are wracked by internal divisions and corruption, and are trying to maintain themselves in a hostile economic and political environment. All this being said, however, it is clear that a number of Marx's predictions about the economic process as it affects capitalists and workers and the structure of capitalism itself were on the mark.

Like Marx, Simmel addressed the issue of social differentiation in society, and in many ways his comments mirror those of Marx. Recall that Simmel visualized modern society as consisting of a large number of variously overlapping social groups or circles. In his discussion of social circles, he argued that often more generalized circles develop out of specialized ones, and noted that the "labor class" is probably the most fascinating example of this process. He sounds very Marxian here: "Independently of what the individual produces, . . . the formal fact that he works for a wage is sufficient to make him a member of a group which includes all those who work under similar conditions. The identical relation to capital permits a differentiation of this similarity out of the different occupations and a combination and union of all those who participate in such a relation." The similar general character of workers' conditions make it possible for them to become integrated into "a unitary class-conscious group."[20] Simmel went on to say that an employer class also develops as a large inclusive social circle encompassing different kinds of employers. But the unification of employers into a large circle occurs more easily, according to Simmel, because the employer's work requires the same *form* (i.e., he or she buys and sells with money) regardless of its *content*. The independence of the form and content of employee work is not as clear, since the form of his or her work depends on the product or content he or she creates.

Since capitalists work with money, they have greater choices and opportunities than workers, since money is a universal medium of exchange and can be used for almost anything. In contrast, workers primarily have only their skills as a commodity and these are more restricted and not as easily exchangeable. This makes workers much less mobile than capitalists, who can use their money anywhere, which means that employers can close up shop and move more easily than employees.

The capitalists' wealth has other advantages, as well. Because there are many arenas in which money can be used, money gives its owner a great deal of prestige. This creates an "unearned increment of wealth." That is, because of their riches, Simmel argued, wealthy people are given advantages and special treatment not accorded the average worker. As shown earlier, the actual "power and significance" of money extends well beyond what the money itself can buy. In this sense, those influences and opportunities are "unearned."[21]

The wealthier employer and poorer employee classes, "placed in formal opposition in relation to each other,"[22] both evolve as capitalism grows into large industry. Large social circles like these classes serve the individual in at least two distinct ways. They allow the person to join with others who have *similar* interests, and the multiplicity and variety of groups also permit the person to develop his or her individuality by having a *unique* combination of memberships. The constant creation and re-creation of new social circles in modern society generates new choices and thereby enhances the freedom of individuals to develop as they wish. In other words, such circles serve both to bring people together and to distinguish them from each other. Cohesiveness and competition are also found together in the social circle. In the case of the employer class, for example, owners join together to protect their common interests, but they also compete with each others as separate employers. This notion of bringing together and separating apart, of collectivity and individuality in the same process, is, of course, a recurrent theme in Simmel's dialectical approach. Here, there are also some similarities to Marx's understanding of social process as the continual confrontation of opposing forces.

ECONOMIC INEQUALITY BETWEEN STATUS GROUPS

The discussion thus far has focused on economic inequality in general. There are also persistent economic discrepancies within the United States between different social categories of people. In 1996, the median income of black and Hispanic households was only 63 and 67 percent, respectively, that of white households. In that same year, over 28 percent of blacks and over 29 percent of Hispanics were classified as poor, compared to just over 11 percent of whites. Moreover, on average, the poor among the former groups are poorer than poor whites. These differences in poverty have persisted for decades, with blacks and Hispanics consistently having rates two to three times those of whites. There are also large differences in income *within* black and Hispanic communities. For example, among blacks in 1996, the bottom 20 percent received only 3.1 percent of all black income, compared to the top 20 percent who possessed 50.7 percent. The share of income owned by the middle groups in the black population has steadily declined since the 1970s. This has caused serious concern among African American scholars who worry that the class differences have become a significant source of division within their racial community. Their concern is part of the larger debate on the relative effects of class and race on the everyday lives of African Americans.

As important as these income differences are, however, there are even larger differences in the wealth of racial and ethnic groups. In 1993, the median net worth of whites was 10 times that of blacks and Hispanics. While the median wealth of whites was over $45,000, that for blacks and Hispanics fell at about $4,500. On the low end of the wealth ladder, one-quarter of black and Hispanic households had zero or negative wealth, compared to only 10 percent of white households. Conversely, at the high end of the wealth hierarchy, about one-third of all white households possessed at least $100,000 in wealth, compared to only 8 percent of blacks and 11 percent of Hispanics.[23]

Significant gaps also exist in earnings between these groups. In 1996, among individuals working full time, year round, the median earnings for whites was $32,966, compared to $26,404 for blacks and $21,056 for Hispanics.[24] Income and earnings discrepancies between these groups persist even after taking into account differences in education, labor-force participation, occupations, and sizes of families. On a variety of measures, then, blacks and Hispanics are significantly less well off financially than whites.

Broader, macroforces appear to be at work in creating economic inequality between the races. Growing intolerance of affirmative action programs among whites and even many African Americans, shifts in the occupational structure, and racial residential segregation have helped maintain racial inequality. As discussed in Chapter 4, racial segregation has concentrated and isolated African Americans within increasingly impoverished settings in which there are mismatches, on the one hand, between the skills held by residents and those demanded in the professional fields, and on the other hand, between where they live and the location of good jobs.

Like racial and ethnic minorities, gender groups differ in their economic statuses. Women are generally less well off economically than men. In 1996, the median income of family households maintained by women was only 60 percent that of male households ($21,564 vs. $35,658). A similar discrepancy existed between men and women living by themselves. The median income of female householders living alone was $14,626, whereas that for comparable males was just over $24,000. Not surprisingly, their wealth also differs. The wealth of married-couple households is over four times that of female-headed households. Most of the wealthiest individuals in the United States are men. On the bottom end, families with female householders are among the families with the highest poverty rates. Married couples had a poverty rate of under 6 percent in 1996; female-headed families had rates approaching 33 percent. Fully 54 percent of all poor families are headed by females with no spouse present. They also tend to be poorer than other poor families, with incomes that fall, on average, $6,657 *below* the poverty line.

Part of the reason for the higher poverty rates among female families is their lower earnings in the job market. In 1996, the median earnings of women who worked full time, year round was $23,710, compared to $32,144 for men in the same category. In every major occupational category and at every educational level, men earn more than women. This is especially true in technical, sales, and craft occupations. The earning differences between these groups declined between the late 1970s and mid-1990s, but it appears that this trend stalled or reversed slightly in the later 1990s.

A major reason given for the decline in income inequality between men and women was declines in the incomes of men rather than rises in the earnings among women. Since the mid-1990s, however, men's earnings are again on the rise, and poorer women are entering the job market, depressing the average wages of women. "There's a growing inequality in the labor market between people at the high end and people at the low end. Women are losing out because more of them are moving into the losing category of lower skilled workers than into the winning categories of highly skilled workers."[25] Part of the explanation for this movement has been the growing impact of recent welfare reform, which pushed more women off welfare into low-paying jobs.

Gender inequality in earnings has little to do with either differences in work interruptions or effort among men and women. Rather, variations in their distributions among occupations is a more significant factor. Occupations that are culturally defined as "female" or "feminine" have lower earnings regardless of who performs them. For example, faculty in nursing, library science, and social work departments, all of which contain a high proportion of women, have significantly lower earnings than professionals in departments with a disproportionate number of men, such as engineering, physics, and dentistry.[26]

ACCOUNTING FOR INEQUALITY
BETWEEN GROUPS

The fact that economic inequality in various forms exists between racial and sex groups—even when differences in education, labor status, family size, occupation, and other *individual* factors are taken into account—suggests that differences in the perceptions of these groups as a whole may explain a significant amount of the inequality that exists. In Chapter 4, I presented Weber's general theory of inequality, within which social status is a crucial component. One of the principal characteristics of a status system are the boundaries that are drawn around groups to distinguish their members from outsiders. From its beginning, race and sex have been important bases of social status boundaries in the United States. In part because of the visible, physical differences between these groups, race and sex have been used traditionally as ways of accounting for variations in behavior, lifestyles, and consumption patterns. Both variables have also been used to justify the unequal treatment of individuals. Clearly, the social status of a group helps us understand its treatment and accomplishments in a society.

As Weber suggested, differences in the treatments of groups are more easily understood and accepted if the underlying differences between the groups are thought to be biological or innate (i.e., if groups are thought of as different "kinds" of people). Race and sex/gender have been traditionally viewed as biologically based variables. If the social and economic inequalities that exist between groups are viewed as being rooted in nature, it is easier to justify them and to maintain the existing social order because it appears to lend scientific weight to the arguments legitimating such inequalities.

Before they colonized the United States, the English afforded blacks lower social status. "Blackness was synonymous with filth, foulness, and evil."[27] Like Native Americans, blacks were viewed as being uncivilized (in European terms). That is, their lifestyle was seen as being deficient or unworthy of social honor, and this in turn suggested that blacks were basically (racially) different from the white colonizers. This made it easier to justify slavery and discriminatory laws that excluded and prevented blacks from succeeding economically and socially. The remnants of this historical discrimination continue to affect relations between blacks and whites even though biological differences are viewed as being less important in explaining differences between races. However, color continues to be a highly significant criterion defining the position of a group in the U.S. ethnic hierarchy. Interracial marriage is still frowned upon and a majority of whites still do not wish to live in heavily mixed neighborhoods. In general, assimilation of African Americans into primary and even secondary relationships with the white majority group continues to be low.

The major reasons appear to have to do primarily with whites' images of blacks' lifestyle and culture. The lack of social mobility among blacks is seen by most whites as being due to group differences in ambition and responsibility (i.e., lifestyle or psychological attributes), rather than to biological inferiority between the races. The most common view among whites, then, is to place the blame for blacks' social and economic situation on their own characteristics rather than to assign blame to innate inferiority, discrimination, or lack of opportunity.[28] This suggests again the low social status that is given to blacks in the United States and the desire on the part of many whites to remain untouched (or uncontaminated) by what they view as the distinctive group behaviors and values of blacks. As ill-advised as it may be, the longing for social purity continues to perpetuate social distance between blacks and whites.

The fact that social status and the honor associated with it are subjectively given by one group to another means that they are rooted in the perceptions and images held of one group by another. The generally negative perceptions of African Americans arise in part from their generally low class position or lack of resources. The clear correlation between race, a nominal category, and economic resources, an ordinal category, leads to a belief in the association between one's race and how far one has gone economically. Since higher amounts of resources are more often found among whites than among blacks, race is thought to be an important reason for resource variations. Consequently, races with lower resources are given lower status than those with higher resources.

As Weber argued, one's status, more frequently than not, is based on one's class position. It is during the process of interaction between individuals from distinctly different racial groups, each of which possess distinctly different levels of resources, that the link is made between one's race and one's status. That is, beliefs are developed about the statuses of different racial groups.[29] Over time, these beliefs develop into an ideology that then shapes and justifies the unequal distribution of resources in society. This ideology is especially important because it justifies the continued monopolization of prized goods, and this monopolization in turn provides strong motivation on the part of higher-status groups to maintain their exclusivity in society. As Weber showed, status groups are distinguished by both their tendencies toward exclusion of outsiders and their monopolization of resources: "For all practical purposes, stratification by status goes hand in hand with the monopolization of ideal and material goods or opportunities, in a manner we have come to know as typical."[30]

The monopolization of desired resources by whites does not allow blacks to progress materially and socially as well as whites. Their resulting poor conditions are then fed into the belief that they are either innately inferior or lack the personal qualities necessary for success. Consequently, in this case, the relationship between ideology and monopolization of goods is reciprocal: Racist ideology justifies exclusion of minorities from valued goods and opportunities, and unequal possession of these goods and opportunities over time reinforces the supposed accuracy of the ideology.

The history of relationships between blacks and whites in the United States is replete with examples of the monopolization of goods and resources by whites, the privileged status group. The rules regarding the rights of slaves provide evidence of the attempts by whites to monopolize valuable resources and thereby to maintain their higher status. Up to the Civil War, for example, black slaves were forbidden to vote, own firearms, own property unless permitted by a master, leave the plantation without permission, and have anyone teach them to read or write. At the turn of the twentieth century, educational opportunities and teachers for blacks were limited and distinctly unequal to those of whites because of their systematic exclusion from voting in southern states. Status is a basis for controlling others. In the South, for instance, the access of blacks to quality education was limited historically. As a coveted good, whites monopolized it to help maintain their higher social status. This illustrates Weber's claim that status is a basis of power. The Jim Crow laws continued this exclusion of blacks from resources by ensuring that blacks and whites remained segregated.[31] In essence, high-status whites were able to use their social status to monopolize important socioeconomic resources and to exclude those of lower social status.

The systematic exclusion of individuals from valuable resources because of their membership in groups of lower status generally occurs without regard for their individual potentials and abilities. It is because of their ascription in a group (e.g., being female or black) that they are excluded, regardless of their personal achievements. Durkheim believed that as modern society progressed, individualism and freedom would become more important as values, and consequently persons would be free to pursue and attain social and occupational positions based on their own personal merits. Being a member of a particular sex or racial group would be less important. Through the implementation of laws that supported their rights and opportunities, Durkheim hoped that the state would create a climate within which individuals could freely and securely operate. Within this protected environment, individual potentials could be realized and placement in social, economic, and political positions would be based on merit rather than group membership. Although there are strains in this direction in modern society, it is clear that group membership or ascription continues to be a basis for attainment. In a word, race and sex still make a significant difference for how far one can get in the division of labor.

In Durkheim's view, the fact that membership in a racial or gender group would significantly affect occupational attainment suggested an abnormal form of the division of labor. Normally, Durkheim believed, the modern division of labor does not operate this way, "but, like all social facts, and, more generally, all biological facts, it presents pathological forms."[32] As in the science of biological forms, the study of these pathological types of the division of labor will allow us to understand better the sources of normality and thereby help us to create a moral division of labor. "Pathology, here as elsewhere, is a valuable aid of physiology."[33]

One explanation that Durkheim provided for the lack of synchronization between various parts of the division of labor is that the rapidity of the detailed large-scale changes that have occurred within it has made coordination or equilibrium in the relationships between parts difficult. New positions and occupations multiply and become part of the division of labor, but the nature of how they should or can be linked to other occupations is not clear. There is not as yet an effective set of rules to structure these relationships in a healthy manner. Consequently, the interpretations and significance of various positions and their connections are not properly understood. For Durkheim, breakdowns in various sectors of the economy provide illustrations of this state of confusion: "They evince, in effect, that at certain points in the organism certain social functions are not adjusted to one another. . . . If the division of labor does not produce solidarity in all these cases, it is because the relations are not regulated, because they are in a state of anomy."[34]

The persistent influence of race and sex as determinants of socioeconomic position might be understood as a product of rapid, unsettling changes in the division of labor. However, the explanation of pathology as residing in an **anomic division of labor** is more appropriate for understanding uncoordinated or imbalanced structural arrangements in the division of labor than for explaining racial and gender inequality. More appropriate is Durkheim's discussion of the **forced division of labor,** a pathological state in which there is a mismatch between individual abilities and the occupational slots people occupy. The rules that govern placement in the division of labor are biased in favor of particular groups who occupy positions in spite of their lack of qualifications for them. The forced division of labor, like its anomic counterpart, is an abnormal but temporary form that Durkheim believed would disappear as industrial society evolved. But in this case, it is not the absence of effective rules but the perverse form that they take that causes the abnormality: "It is not sufficient that there be rules, however, for sometimes the rules themselves are the cause of evil. . . . The institution of classes and of castes constitutes an organization of the division of labor, and it is a strictly regulated organization, although it often is a source of dissension."[35]

As is typical of status-group processes, some groups are excluded from performing certain functions in the division of labor. But for it to perform efficiently and morally, there must be a fit between the abilities of the individual and the functions he or she performs. A lack of fit arising from the exclusion of some groups leads to a lack of solidarity in society "because the distribution of social functions . . . does not respond, or rather no longer responds, to the distribution of natural talents."[36] It is the lack of natural fit that would result from the free flow of talent throughout society that causes Durkheim to refer to this aberrant form as "forced."

Individual freedom requires that these artificial arrangements be changed, and Durkheim felt they would be changed as social forces in the evolution of society take hold more fully. This means that, from Durkheim's perspective, modern society will progressively move toward greater justice through the free flowering of individual talents. Individuals will be able to be "all that they can be." When we look at society today, however, it is apparent that we still have a long way to go. Durkheim rightly saw justice as a *task* for modern societies, but his emphasis on the natural, evolutionary manner in which such justice would appear probably underestimates the difficulty of that task.

CONCLUSION

There is abundant evidence that economic inequality has increased in the United States in recent decades, and that particular groups have suffered disproportionately in the process. Many of these groups (e.g., women and African Americans) have been denied opportunities and resources throughout their histories. In this chapter, I have tried to demonstrate the magnitude of economic and intergroup inequalities and the direct relevance of the ideas of classical theorists in making sense of them. Their theories are not always fully adequate in accounting for specific details or nuances within contemporary society, but the overall thrust and major concepts in their arguments illuminate many, if not most, of the broad features of inequality in the United States. The central ideas used from their perspectives are included in Comparative Chart 7.1.

Certainly, Marx's depiction of the internal operation of capitalism locates critical foci of class processes that still affect relationships between workers and employers and the distribution of economic rewards. Simmel, as well, realized that broad similarities among individuals can bring them together as a group at the same time that differences between them can separate them as individuals. Capitalists in general have an advantage over workers because they deal in money rather than in skills, and the money form has a liquidity that skills lack. This gives capitalists a greater range of opportunities than workers. Weber's theory of social status is directly relevant for an understanding of the treatment of

COMPARATIVE CHART 7.1   Basic Ideas from Each Theorist Used in Analyses of Chapter Issues

	Economic Inequality in General	Economic Inequality between Groups
Marx	Class as relationship to means of production; three main classes and historical shifts in class relationships and structure; stages of capitalism and corporate trends; alienating effects of division of labor; overproduction crises; development of workers from class-in-itself to class-for-itself; centralization of capital	
Durkheim		Movement toward merit-based occupational placement in modern society; state as protector of individual; anomic and forced divisions of labor as temporary aberrations; justice as a task of modern society
Simmel	Labor class as social circle and class-conscious group based on working for wage; capitalists as social circle unified by common use of money as a universal medium of exchange; workers as less mobile than capitalists; power and prestige of money; opposition of workers and capitalists; class circles as bases for group cohesion and individual expressiveness	
Weber		Race and sex as bases of status boundaries; status group characteristics of racial and gender groups; blacks and women as different kinds of people; denigration of life-styles and culture of blacks; status prestige/honor as based on class; reciprocal relationship between ideology and the monopolization of resources

individuals in different social categories. It is particularly his identification of monopolization and exclusion that helps us in understanding the lower status of women and minorities.

Finally, Durkheim hoped that this lower group status would be eliminated in time, but he also realized that while developing toward a more perfect state, modern societies go through aberrations in which many individuals and groups are discriminated against. An underriding theme of all their arguments is that of the exclusion of some groups by others. On this basis, social inequality is much more a source of division than unity in the United States today.

QUESTIONS TO PONDER

1. What are the most insightful or useful measures of class position? Why? How does inequality on each of these measures affect the lives of individuals?

2. What evidence is there to assess the adequacy and/or inadequacy of Marx's predictions about the relationship between workers and large employers?

3. What parallels exist in the ideologies used to maintain different racial and gender categories as separate status groups? What is your position on Durkheim's prediction that the use of race and gender for positioning individuals in occupations will be eliminated someday?

A SUMMING UP

I began this book by showing the concrete importance of social theory, and specifically the continuing relevance of Marx, Weber, Simmel, and Durkheim for understanding issues related to integration and disintegration in the contemporary United States. Having lived through early industrialization and calamitous social and political changes in their own countries, these thinkers were unavoidably interested in understanding the inner workings of modern Western society and its evolution. Though different in their emphases and conclusions, all four theorists identified sources of cohesion and divisiveness in modern society.

Marx's detailed analyses of capitalism's structure and the processes at work within it help us make sense of the broad, significant changes occurring in the economy. These events aid in understanding the alienation of many who are excluded from the bounty of capitalism. Among other things, the operation of capitalism accounts, in part, for the existence of walled communities and ghettos, widespread political distrust and cynicism, and growing economic inequality in the United States. It helps us understand the conflict between the individual, on the one hand, and society as it is presently structured, on the other.

The rationalization of modern Western society, as envisioned by Weber, proceeded apace throughout most of the twentieth century, and has enveloped many institutions and formed the basis of a dominant mindset in our society. This is manifested in the emphases placed on rational behavior, objectivity, calculation, efficiency, science, and technology. Weber realized that although all of these enable us to reach ends more effectively, none of these can provide us with values by which to live. Science, money, and technology can be used for any number of purposes. Science can be used for self-aggrandizement, as in cosmetic plastic surgery or increasing life expectancy. Computers can be used to invade the privacy of others or enrich our social relationships. Money can be used to buy elections or help others. Bureaucracy can be used for selfish or collective ends. What modern society requires and what it lacks is a set of ultimate human values to guide its destiny.

Weber and Marx both saw society as being plagued by different forms of inequality. Economics, race, and gender divide U.S. society and too often break its people into warring or at least distant camps. Along with Simmel, both scholars forecast the commodification of an increasing number of objects and persons in modern society.

Simmel's own interpretation of modern culture and society was ambivalent. For better or for worse, individuals and society are irrevocably tied together. Each needs the other. He understood the freedom and individuality that money and contemporary cities could offer, but was also aware of the problems that attended the dominance of money and larger size and heterogeneity in cities. Marx, Weber, and Simmel were all sensitive to the power of money to divide people, distort communication, corrupt values, and dissolve meaningful qualitative differences. In Simmel's vision, cities often end up being spatially organized into bounded areas occupied by different social and economic groups.

Finally, Durkheim's perspective of evolving industrial society identified the division of labor as a major source of social integration. At the same time, he argued that egoism and individuality would continue to increase, creating a more intense conflict between individuals and their moral ties to others. The difficulties caused by the lack of an abiding and widespread secular morality include various types of injustice, including political corruption and social distrust, economic inequality between groups, and the adoration of the body over higher values. At the same time, Durkheim was aware that the sacred element in social life continues in industrial society, even though its content and the objects of our adoration may change. He was optimistic about the prospects of modern Western societies such as the United States becoming increasingly just and civilized.

The worlds described by the classical theorists have changed and not changed. Modern industrial societies still have most of the central features identified by these thinkers: bureaucracies, classes, cities, and divisions of labor. In addition, the dilemmas rooted in social diversity and the individual/society relationship continue—as do many of the underlying processes identified by them that divide and/or unite us.

Still, some significant alterations have occurred in the United States since the classical theorists wrote. Most notably have been qualitative leaps in science and information technology. These changes have the potential to reshape our lives and their meaning, as well as our relationships with others. Among the specific changes are medical and technological breakthroughs. Human cloning is now at least theoretically possible and raises ethical questions about the nature and value of human life. Genetic research has also progressed to the point where some are convinced that not only will much behavior be explained biologically but that morality itself may have a biological source.[1]

Computer and photographic technologies have progressed at a pace that only 10 to 20 years ago was considered unimaginable. This technology has made the distinction between fact and fiction less firm. Digital technology in photography allows the creation of pictures whose content is fictitious. What is on film can lie. Perhaps we have entered an "age of falsification."[2] Computers create virtual worlds, also unreal in a traditional sense, into which users can escape. The information highway brings us all closer together, or at least more accessible to each other.

The classical theorists were well aware of the power and possibilities of modern technology, but it is unlikely that they anticipated the magnitude and pace of the changes that are occurring as we enter the twenty-first century. One debatable issue is whether these changes are merely new wrinkles or trappings in *modern* societies that remain fundamentally the same structurally, or whether we have entered a qualitatively different *postmodern* society and culture. A critical question remains: Are the problems of alienation and disunity discussed in these pages bellwethers for what awaits us?

GLOSSARY OF CLASSICAL THEORETICAL TERMS

Note: The theorist with whom the concept is usually associated is shown in parentheses.

affective action: an action or behavior motivated by emotions and done for its own sake (Weber).

alienation: primarily a structural condition but also a feeling in which the individual is unnaturally separated from others, products of labor, labor process, and/or self (Marx).

altruistic suicide: conscious self-destruction caused by the extreme identification with and integration of the individual into a group or society (Durkheim).

anomic division of labor: an abnormal but temporary form of the division of labor resulting from the ineffective regulation of the coordination of occupational positions, and due primarily to the degree and rapidity of change and complexity in the economic structure (Durkheim).

anomic suicide: self-destruction caused by a lack of effective collective regulation or normative constraint of the individual (Durkheim).

anomie: a structural condition in which effective established rules for social behavior are absent, resulting in a lack of guidance and limits for individuals (Durkheim).

blasé attitude: a matter-of-fact, cool, unconcerned attitude adopted by urbanites as a response to overstimulation (Simmel).

bureaucracy: a type of formal organizational structure noted for its impersonality and characterized by a defined division of labor, hierarchy of authority, written communication, professional expertise, and a career system (Weber).

capitalism: an economic system that is characterized by private property, a free labor market, and oriented toward the enhancement of private profit (Marx).

centrifugal forces: social, economic, political, and/or cultural processes and institutions that pull society outward or increase social distance between its components (Simmel).

centripetal forces: social, economic, political, and/or cultural processes and institutions that draw society's components toward each other and generally enhance cohesion and integration in society (Simmel).

charismatic authority: the accepted power of an individual that is based on and legitimated by qualities of personality (Weber).

charismatic organizations: organizations that are structured around a powerful personality or leader and thus are not rationally structured like a bureaucracy or organized according to tradition or custom (Weber).

class: a market position in the economic order generally determined by property ownership or skills (Weber); a person's position in relationship to the means of economic production (Marx).

class-for-itself: a class that has the characteristics of a group and is conscious of its position vis-à-vis another class, and is politically organized to fight for its interests (Marx).

class-in-itself: a nonorganized aggregate of individuals who are in the same objective position in relation to the means of production (Marx).

collective conscience: an underlying, commonly held set of beliefs and values that exist as a social fact independent of particular individuals, that constrains them, and that helps hold a society together (Durkheim).

communist society: characterized by the absences of private property, alienation, a fixed division of labor, and a class-biased government (Marx).

corporate group: a group of individuals with the same occupation that provides the rules and ethics by which individuals in that occupation operate and relate to other groups in society (Durkheim).

dialectic: the notion that change in a system is brought about by its own internal contradictions, such as between the means and relations of production (Marx); the process of blending opposing—positive and negative, integrating and disintegrating—forces (Simmel).

division of labor: a formal structure of work or occupational specialization (Durkheim, Marx).

economic order: that part of the structure of society involving the distribution pattern of goods and services, and that includes hierarchically arranged classes differentiated by their market situation (Weber).

egoistic suicide: results when the individual is not sufficiently socially integrated into society—that is, the person lacks a network of social support (Durkheim).

fatalistic suicide: results from the absence of opportunities to escape the crushing overregulation of society on the individual (Durkheim).

forced division of labor: a pathological form of the division of labor in which the rules governing access to occupational positions result in a mismatch between the positions held and individual abilities (Durkheim).

formal rationality: an instrumental orientation or mental framework in which the emphasis in behavior is placed solely on the most effective means to reach an end regardless of the quality or value of that end (Weber).

forms: structures or modes created in interaction that are analytically distinct from their content (Simmel).

ideology: an organized set of beliefs aimed at justifying existing or alternate social arrangements (Marx).

integration: the coordination or interconnecting of various parts, including individuals and groups, of a social system in an effective manner (Durkheim).

iron cage: the increasingly rational structure of modern life that hems in human beings (Weber).

legal-rational authority: domination that is considered acceptable on the basis of one's legitimately obtained formal position or office (Weber).

moral behavior: behavior that is disciplined, autonomous, and oriented toward the collectivity (Durkheim).

moral individualism: an enlightened principle or form of individualism in which individuals take into account and honor the individuality of others; to be constrasted with "egoistic individualism," which focuses sole concern on one's own interests (Durkheim).

nonrational action: includes action or behavior that is emotionally rooted and taken for its own sake or motivated by tradition (Weber).

objective culture: those human products and objects that take on a power and life of their own far removed from the creative human impulse that originally gave rise to them (Simmel).

objective spirit: the ambience or cultural condition in the city created by a dominance of rational elements such as intellect, quantification, calculation, and punctuality (Simmel).

party: a group organized to enhance its political power; can be based on any number of socioeconomic characteristics that individuals share, including class and status (Weber).

patrimonial organizations: organizations that are structured and administered according to traditional norms and personal loyalty instead of formal rational criteria (Weber).

political order: that dimension of the societal structure pertaining to the organization of parties and political power (Weber).

profane: pertaining to that sphere of life rooted in human beings as organisms and involving the everyday, earthy, material elements of mundane living; separate from and opposed to the sacred sphere of life (Durkheim).

Protestant ethic: a religiously based, severe, ascetic approach to life that stresses unremitting hard work, refraining from sensual enjoyment, and success in the eyes of God (Weber).

purposively rational action: a behavior or action that is taken in which there is a conscious attempt to select from among alternatives the most efficient and effective means to some goal, which in itself may also be viewed as a means to another goal (Weber).

rationalization: concerns the impersonal, objective, scientific, economic, and technical (i.e., overly rational) quality of modern society; associated with the disenchantment of modern life (Weber).

routinization of charisma: the transformation and stabilization of authority originally based on personal qualities into authority based on either tradition or formal position (Weber).

sacred: that sphere of life derived from social life that incorporates all the so-called higher elements of life, such as reason, morality, science, sociality, conceptualizations, and the soul; distinct from and opposed to the profane sphere of life (Durkheim).

secular morality: rather than focusing on the supernatural, this is a morality that emphasizes the importance of nurturing one's relationships to others and developing the social side of one's nature (Durkheim).

social facts: aspects and dimensions of social reality that exist on a separate plane; that cannot be reduced to psychological, biological, or physical phenomena; and that have a constraining effect on individuals (Durkheim).

social order: that component of the structure of a society pertaining primarily to the distribution of status honor among groups (Weber).

social status: the degree of honor or prestige subjectively accorded an individual or group by a community (Weber).

species-being: an individual's basic commonality with others in the human species; humans' essential social nature (Marx).

status group: a group accorded a positive or negative degree of prestige or social honor by a community and distinguished by a separate lifestyle, level of intimacy, and separated by a social boundary from outsiders (Weber).

subjective culture: the dynamic expressive act of human creativity, a characteristic of actual life rather than objectivized form (Simmel).

substantive rationality: pertaining to behavior that is oriented toward deeply held ultimate values, thus giving it significant meaning (Weber).

substructure: the economic basis or foundation on which the rest of society or superstructure is finally built; the mode of production in a society (Marx).

superstructure: the noneconomic components of a society's structure and culture that reflect its substructure, including social, political, religious, and educational institutions along with their ideological elements (Marx).

totemic symbols: material objects that are the concrete representations of sacred meanings in a group or society, such as a national flag (Durkheim).

traditional action: behavior that is directed by tradition or custom rather than by conscious calculation or emotion (Weber).

traditional authority: domination that has been legitimated based on tradition or custom, such as patriarchalism, in which the father is accepted as the head of the household (Weber).

value-rational action: goal-oriented behavior in which means are rationally chosen for their effectiveness in reaching an end that is based on what one deeply values (Weber).

Chapter 1

1. The expert referred to is James Alan Fox, cited in Julie Stacey, "The Dean of Death," *USA Today,* April 11, 1995: 1A–2A. The statistics are from U.S. Department of Justice, Bureau of Justice Statistics, 1996, *Sourcebook of Criminal Justice Statistics—1995* (Washington, DC: U.S. Government Printing Office, 1996), p. 403.
2. Ibid., p. 129.
3. See, for example, the entire issues of *Commentary,* November 1995, and *The Public Interest,* Winter 1997.
4. Charles Derber, *The Wilding of America* (New York: St. Martin's, 1996).
5. Ibid., p. 9.
6. U.S. Department of Justice, *Criminal Justice Statistics—1995,* p. 132; James A. Davis and Tom W. Smith, *General Social Surveys, 1972–1996: Cumulative Codebook* (Chicago: National Opinion Research Center, 1996), p. 190.
7. I am, of course, assuming here that reality exists *outside* theories, and is not merely a creation or reflection of them or identical with them. There is a debate, especially in postmodernist circles, about the value of broad "grand narrative" theories and about the existence of reality/realities as independent from the words used to describe it/them. But it is not my purpose to pursue this debate here, so I am just mentioning it.
8. Georgie Anne Geyer, *Americans No More* (New York: Atlantic Monthly Press, 1996).
9. The brief historical sketches of France and Germany draw heavily from J. P.

T. Bury, *France 1814–1940* (London: Methuen, 1985); Roger Magraw, *France 1815–1914* (New York: Oxford, 1983); E. J. Passant, *A Short History of Germany, 1815–1945* (Cambridge: Cambridge University Press, 1959); and Helmut Walser Smith, *German Nationalism and Religious Conflict* (Princeton, NJ: Princeton University Press, 1995).
10. Robert N. Bellah (ed.), *Emile Durkheim: On Morality and Society* (Chicago: University of Chicago Press, 1973), p. 139.
11. Georg Simmel, *Conflict* and *The Web of Group-Affiliations* (Glencoe, IL: Free Press, 1955), p. 15.
12. David Frisby, *Simmel and Since: Essays on Georg Simmel's Social Theory* (London: Routledge, 1992), p. 69.
13. Kurt H. Wolff (ed.), *The Sociology of Georg Simmel* (New York: Free Press, 1950), p. 97.
14. Jim Faught, "Neglected Affinities: Max Weber and Georg Simmel," *British Journal of Sociology,* 1985, vol. 36, pp. 155–74.
15. H. H. Gerth and C. Wright Mills (eds.), *From Max Weber: Essays in Sociology* (New York: Oxford, 1946), p. 155.
16. Ibid., p. 214.
17. Ibid., p. 216.

Chapter 2

1. Since the aim of this book is to apply the ideas of classical theorists to the contemporary United States, I am focusing on modern *Western* society rather than on modern society in general. The classical theorists generally

equated modernization with Westernization, although today it is recognized that modernization does not necessarily mean Westernization.

2. T. B. Bottomore and Maximilien Rubel (eds.), *Karl Marx: Selected Writings in Sociology and Social Philosophy* (New York: McGraw-Hill, 1964), p. 97.

3. Georg Simmel, *The Philosophy of Money* (Boston: Routledge, 1978), p. 297.

4. Simmel, *Philosophy of Money*, p. 454.

5. Emile Durkheim, *The Division of Labor* (New York: The Free Press, 1933), p. 403.

6. Thomas Dye, *Who's Running America?: The Clinton Years* (Englewood Cliffs, NJ: Prentice-Hall, 1995).

7. Bottomore and Rubel, *Karl Marx*, p. 128.

8. Ruth Wallace, "Emile Durkheim and the Civil Religion Concept," *Review of Religious Research,* 1977: 287–90.

9. Bryan Appleyard, Martin Marty, Daniel Boorstin, and Munawar Ahmad Anees, "Progress of Faith, Retreat of Reason?" *New Perspectives Quarterly,* Summer 1993: 52–59.

10. Max Weber, *The Protestant Ethic and the Spirit of Capitalism* (Los Angeles: Roxbury, 1996), p. 181.

11. Ibid., p. 182.

12. Emile Durkheim, "Individualism and the Intellectuals," in R. N. Bellah (ed.), *Emile Durkheim: On Morality and Society* (Chicago: University of Chicago, 1973), p. 52.

13. Lynn Elber, "Do TV Journalists Threaten Credibility with Movie Roles?" *Akron Beacon Journal,* June 12, 1997: E1.

14. See, for example, Deena Weinstein and Michael A. Weinstein, "Simmel and the Theory of Postmodern Society," in B. S. Turner (ed.), *Theories of Modernity and Postmodernity* (New-

bury Park, CA: Sage), pp. 75–87; David Frisby, *Simmel and Since: Essays on Georg Simmel's Social Theory* (London: Routledge); and Gary D. Jaworski, *Georg Simmel and the American Prospect* (Albany: State University of New York, 1997).

15. Mustafa Emirbayer, "Useful Durkheim," *Sociological Theory,* July 1996: 110–130; and Stjepan G. Mestrovic, *The Coming Fin de Siecle* (London: Routledge, 1991).

16. Quote from Hans H. Gerth, "Max Weber: A Man Under Stress," in Peter Hamilton (ed.), *Max Weber: Critical Assessments,* vol. 1 (London: Routledge, 1991), pp. 40–44.

17. Lewis Coser, *Masters of Sociological Thought* (New York: Harcourt, 1971), p. 173.

18. Durkheim, *Division of Labor,* pp. 79, 181.

19. Terry Pluto, "Springer Ahead? Hardly," *Akron Beacon Journal,* March 10, 1998: C6.

20. Ibid.

21. See Emile Durkheim, *The Elementary Forms of Religious Life* (New York: Free Press, 1965), especially the Conclusion.

22. Durkheim, *Division of Labor,* p. 401.

23. Ibid., p. 37.

24. Emile Durkheim, *Suicide* (New York: Free Press), Chapters 2 and 3.

25. Durkheim, *Division of Labor,* p. 28.

26. Karl Marx and Friedrich Engels, *The Communist Manifesto* (New York: Bantam, 1992), pp. 19–20.

27. Robert C. Tucker (ed.), *The Marx-Engels Reader* (New York: Norton, 1978), p. 172.

28. Jean-Pierre Berlan, "The Commodification of Life," *Monthy Review,* December 1989: 24–30.

29. See Mary E. Virnoche and Gary T. Marx, "'Only Connect'—E. M. Forster in an Age of Electronic Communica-

tion: Computer-Mediated Association and Community Networks," *Sociological Inquiry,* February 1997: 85–100; Kristen Purcell, "Towards a Communication Dialectic: Embedded Technology and the Enhancement of Place," *Sociological Inquiry,* February 1997: 101–112; and Claude S. Fischer, "Technology and Community: Historical Complexities," *Sociological Inquiry,* February 1997: 113–118.

30. Simmel, *Philosophy of Money.* In addition to money and the other factors discussed, Simmel also identified various patterns of superordination and subordination as sources of integration and disintegration. Although such hierarchies separate people, they also bind people together. Subordinates, for example, can be tied together in their common devotion to the person on top, but their devotion can also create competition and jealousy between them, driving them apart.

31. Kurt H. Wolff (ed.), *The Sociology of Georg Simmel* (New York: Free Press, 1950), p. 88.

32. Ibid., p. 20.

Chapter 3

1. Cornel West, *Race Matters* (New York: Vintage), pp. 11, 13.

2. R. L. Stevenson, *Dr. Jekyll and Mr. Hyde* (Hertfordshire, England: Wordsworth, 1993), pp. 43, 44–45.

3. Robert N. Bellah (ed.), *Emile Durkheim On Morality and Society* (Chicago: University of Chicago, 1973), p. 157.

4. Ibid., p. 163.

5. For Simmel's views of human nature, see Jorge Arditi, "Simmel's Theory of Alienation and the Decline of the Non-rational," *Sociological Theory,* July 1996: 95; Georg Simmel, *Conflict* and

The Web of Group-Affiliations (Glencoe, IL: Free Press, 1955); and Donald N. Levine (ed.), *George Simmel On Individuality and Social Forms* (Chicago: University of Chicago, 1971).

6. T. B. Bottomore and Maximilien Rubel (eds.), *Karl Marx: Selected Readings in Sociology and Social Philosophy* (New York: McGraw-Hill, 1964), pp. 68, 77.

7. Tom Campbell, *Seven Theories of Human Society* (Oxford: Clarendon, 1981).

8. Georg Simmel, *The Philosophy of Money* (Boston: Routledge, 1978), p. 494.

9. Bellah, *Emile Durkheim,* pp. 48–49; see also Lise Ann Tole, "Durkheim on Religion and Moral Community in Modernity," *Sociological Inquiry,* February 1993: 1–29.

10. Lance Morrow, "A Nation of Finger Pointers," *Time,* August 12, 1991: 15.

11. See the website for the Association for California Tort Reform: www.sna.com/actr/2000/stop.html

12. Amitai Etzioni, "Crimes Against the People," *Utne Reader,* March/April, 1993: 74–75.

13. Philip A. Mellor and Chris Shilling, "Modernity, Self-Identity and the Sequestration of Death," *Sociology,* August 1993: 417, 427.

14. Georg Simmel, *Philosophy of Money,* pp. 298, 437.

15. Amitai Etzioni, "A New Community of Thinkers, Both Liberal and Conservative," *Wall Street Journal,* October 8, 1991: 22.

16. Ibid.

17. Arno Penzias, "Technology and the Rest of Culture," *Social Research,* Fall 1997: 1035.

18. Ibid., pp. 1034–35, 1038–39.

19. Ibid., p. 1041.

20. Malcolm R. Parks and Kory Floyd, "Making Friends in Cyberspace,"

Journal of Communication, Winter 1996: 80–97.

21. Amy Harmon, "On-Line Trail to an Off-Line Killing," *New York Times,* April 30, 1998: A30.

22. Ibid.

23. Mindy Charski, "Now on the Net: Live Birth. Next: the Operating Room," *U.S. News & World Report,* June 29, 1998: 36.

24. Rebecca Piirto Heath, "Tuning in to Talk," *American Demographics,* February 1998: 48–49.

25. Nina Bernstein, "On Line, High-Tech Sleuths Find Private Facts," *New York Times,* September 15, 1997: A1.

26. Ibid.

27. Ibid.

28. Max Weber, *The Protestant Ethic and the Spirit of Capitalism* (Los Angeles: Roxbury, 1996), p. 17.

29. Emile Durkheim, *Suicide* (New York: Free Press, 1951).

30. Ibid., p. 209.

31. John P. D'Attilio, Brian M. Campbell, Pierre Lubold, Tania Jacobson, and Julie A. Richard, "Social Support and Suicide Potential: Preliminary Findings for Adolescent Populations," *Psychological Reports,* vol. 70, 1992: 76–78; and David Lester, "Social Correlates of Youth Suicide Rates in the United States," *Adolescence,* Spring 1991: 55–57.

32. Pam Belluck, "Black Youths' Rate of Suicide Rising Sharply, Studies Find," *New York Times,* March 20, 1998: A1, A16.

33. West, *Race Matters,* p. 23.

34. Ian Craib, *Classical Social Theory* (Oxford: Oxford, 1997).

Chapter 4

1. Donald N. Levine (ed.), *Georg Simmel On Individuality and Social Forms* (Chicago: University of Chicago, 1971), p. 24.

2. Ibid., p. 376–77.

3. Ibid., p. 391.

4. Ibid., p. xvii.

5. Nicholas J. Spykman, *The Social Theory of Georg Simmel* (New York: Atherton, 1966), pp. 144–45.

6. Mark Abrahamson, *Urban Enclaves: Identity and Place in America* (New York: St. Martin's, 1996), p. 19.

7. Spykman, *Georg Simmel,* p. 148.

8. Edward J. Blakely and Mary Gail Snyder, *Fortress America: Gated Communities in the United States* (Washington, DC: Brookings and Cambridge, MA: Lincoln Institute of Land Policy, 1997), p. 1.

9. Georg Simmel, *Conflict* and *The Web of Group-Affiliations* (Glencoe, IL: Free Press, 1955), p. 137.

10. Floyd Hunter, *Community Power Structure: A Study of Decision Makers* (Chapel Hill: University of North Carolina, 1953).

11. Lawrence A. Scaff, "Social Theory, Rationalism and the Architecture of the City: Fin-de-siecle Thematics," *Theory, Culture & Society,* vol. 12, 1995: 64–65.

12. Peter Marcuse, "The Enclave, the Citadel, and the Ghetto: What Has Changed in the Post-Fordist U.S. City," *Urban Affairs Review,* November 1997: 228–64.

13. Blakely and Snyder, *Fortress America.*

14. Ibid., p. 2.

15. Abrahamson, *Urban Enclaves,* p. 2.

16. Frank Heflin, "Closed Gates Trouble Outsiders," *The Progressive,* October 1993: 32.

17. Blakely and Snyder, *Fortress America,* p. 30.

18. H. H. Gerth and C. Wright Mills (eds.), *From Max Weber* (New York: Oxford, 1962), p. 190.

19. "Government by the Nice, for the Nice," *The Economist,* July 25, 1992: 26.

20. Blakely and Snyder, *Fortress America,* p. 145.

21. Gerth and Mills, *From Max Weber,* p. 191.

22. Ibid., p. 186; italics mine.

23. Blakely and Snyder, *Fortress America.*

24. Gerth and Mills, *From Max Weber,* p. 188.

25. Max Weber, *Economy and Society* (New York: Bedminster, 1968), p. 307.

26. Peter Cookson, Jr. and Caroline Hodges Persell, *Preparing for Power: America's Elite Boarding Schools* (New York: Basic, 1985).

27. Stephen Richard Higley, *Privilege, Power, and Place* (Lanham, MD: Rowman & Littlefield, 1995).

28. Ibid.

29. Abrahamson, *Urban Enclaves.*

30. Ibid., p. 25.

31. Ibid.

32. T. B. Bottomore and Maximilien Rubel (eds.), *Karl Marx: Selected Writings in Sociology and Social Philosophy* (New York: McGraw-Hill, 1964), p. 99.

33. Ibid., p. 54.

34. Martin N. Marger, *Race and Ethnic Relations: American and Global Perspectives* (Belmont, CA: Wadsworth, 1997), p. 260.

35. Douglas S. Massey and Nancy A. Denton, *American Apartheid* (Cambridge, MA: Harvard, 1993).

36. Ibid., p. 77.

37. Marcuse, "The Enclave, the Citadel, and the Ghetto"; and William J. Wilson, *The Truly Disadvantaged: The Inner City, the Underclass, and Public Policy* (Chicago: University of Chicago, 1987).

38. Melvin L. Oliver and Thomas M. Shapiro, *Black Wealth/White Wealth* (New York: Routledge, 1995).

39. Ibid.

40. William W. Goldsmith and Edward J. Blakely, *Separate Societies* (Philadelphia: Temple, 1992), pp. 111, 125.

41. Claudia J. Coulton, Julian Chow, Edward C. Wang, and Marilyn Su, "Geographic Concentration of Affluence and Poverty in 100 Metropolitan Areas, 1990," *Urban Affairs Review,* November 1996: 186–216.

42. Douglas S. Massey, Andrew B. Gross, and Kumiko Shibuya, "Migration, Segregation, and the Geographic Segregation of Poverty," *American Sociological Review,* June 1994: 425–45.

43. Massey and Denton, *American Apartheid;* and Marger, *Race and Ethnic Relations.*

44. See Massey and Denton, *American Apartheid,* pp. 88–95 for a summary of studies.

45. Ibid., p. 94.

46. Gerth and Mills, *From Max Weber,* p. 188.

47. See, for example, Gunnar Myrdal, *An American Dilemma: The Negro Problem and Modern Democracy* (New York: Harper, 1944); Gerald D. Berreman, "Caste in India and the United States," *American Journal of Sociology,* vol. 66, 1960: 120–27; and Charles V. Willie, *The Caste and Class Controversy* (Bayside, NY: General Hall, 1979).

48. Gerth and Mills, *From Max Weber,* p. 190.

49. John Stone, "Race, Ethnicity, and the Weberian Legacy," *American Behavioral Scientist,* January 1995: 391–406.

50. W. E. B. DuBois, *An ABC of Color* (New York: International, 1969).

51. Gerth and Mills, *From Max Weber,* pp. 16–17.

52. Ibid., p. 180.

53. Massey and Denton, *American Apartheid,* p. 111.

Chapter 5

1. Caroline Hodges Persell, "The Interdependence of Social Justice and Civil Society," *Sociological Forum,* vol. 12, 1997: 150.
2. See James Allan Davis and Tom W. Smith, *General Social Surveys, 1972–1996*. Principal Investigator, James A. Davis; Director and Co-Principal Investigator, Tom W. Smith. NORC ed. (Chicago: National Opinion Research Center, producer, 1996, and Storrs, CT: The Roper Center for Public Opinion Research, University of Connecticut, distributor; George Gallup, Jr., *The Gallup Poll: Public Opinion 1996,* Wilmington, DE: Scholarly Resources, Inc., 1996).
3. Gallup, *The Gallop Poll;* and for a review of myths about the 1950s, see Stephanie Coontz, *The Way We Never Were* (New York: Basic, 1992).
4. Robert A. Campbell and James E. Curtis, "The Public's Views on the Future of Religion and Science: Cross-National Survey Results," *Review of Religious Research,* March 1996: 260–267.
5. Tom W. Smith (ed.), *GSS News,* August 1997 (Chicago: National Opinion Research Center, 1997); and Davis and Smith, *General Social Surveys.*
6. David R. Simon and D. Stanley Eitzen, *Elite Deviance* (Boston: Allyn and Bacon, 1993), p. 2.
7. This discussion of the savings and loan scandal relies heavily on the readings in Robert Emmet Long (ed.), *Banking Scandals: The S & Ls and BCCI,* The Reference Shelf, vol. 65, no. 3 (New York: H. W. Wilson, 1993).
8. Robert Williams, "Private Interests and Public Office: The American Experience of Sleaze," *Parliamentary Affairs,* October 1995: 632.
9. Lydia Saad, "Public Has Low Expectations of Campaign Finance Investigation," *The Gallup Poll Monthly,* August 1997: 13–14.
10. Hugh Heclo, "The Sixties' False Dawn: Awakenings, Movements, and Postmodern Policy-making," *Journal of Policy History,* vol. 8, no. 1, 1996: 57–58.
11. Ibid.
12. Dirk Johnson, "Civility in Politics: Going, Going, Gone," *New York Times,* December 10, 1997: A14.
13. F. Richard Ciccone, "Truth Hard to Discern in America," *Akron Beacon Journal,* June 23, 1996: G3.
14. Jeff Goldberg, "Truth & Consequences," *Omni,* November 1990: 72+; see also Zina Sawaya, "Getting Even," *Forbes,* April 29, 1991: 92–95; Scott Shuger, "Public Eye," *New York Times Magazine,* September 13, 1992: 57+.
15. Eric W. Rothenbuhler, Lawrence J. Mullen, Richard DeLaurell, and Choon Ryul Ryu, "Communication, Community Attachment, and Involvement," *Journalism & Mass Communication Quarterly,* Summer 1996: 445–66.
16. Robert N. Bellah (ed.), *Emile Durkheim On Morality and Society* (Chicago: University of Chicago, 1973), pp. 154, 157.
17. John C. Bollens and Henry J. Schmandt, *Political Corruption: Power, Money, and Sex* (Pacific Palisades, CA: Palisades Publishers, 1979).
18. Bellah, *Emile Durkheim,* p. 133.
19. Emile Durkheim, *Moral Education* (New York: Free Press, 1961), p. 37.
20. Ibid., p. 40.
21. Ibid., p. 59.
22. Ibid., p. 71.
23. Ibid., p. 17.
24. Frank Newport, "Small Business and Military Generate Most Confidence in Americans," *The Gallup Poll Monthly,*

August 1997: 21–24; and Davis and Smith, *General Social Surveys.*

25. Max Weber, *Economy and Society,* vol. 3 (New York: Bedminster, 1968), p. 975.
26. It is interesting that both Durkheim and Weber stress the importance of impersonality in mitigating selfish behavior, although Durkheim cites the impersonal nature of morality and Weber emphasizes the impersonality of bureaucracy.
27. Weber, *Economy and Society,* p. 1010.
28. H. H. Gerth and C. Wright Mills, *From Max Weber* (New York: Oxford, 1962), pp. 229–30.
29. Ibid., p. 231.
30. Arthur G. Emig, Michael B. Hesse, and Samuel H. Fisher, III, "Black-White Differences in Political Efficacy, Trust, and Sociopolitical Participation: A Critique of the Empowerment Hypothesis," *Urban Affairs Review,* November 1996: 264–76.
31. Gerth and Mills, *From Max Weber,* p. 230.
32. Larry Makinson and Joshua Goldstein, *Open Secrets: The Encyclopedia of Congressional Money and Politics* (Washington, DC: Congressional Quarterly, 1994).
33. Viviana A. Zelizer, *The Social Meaning of Money* (New York: Basic, 1994).
34. Georg Simmel, *The Philosophy of Money* (Boston: Routledge, 1978), p. 497.
35. Ibid., p. 257.
36. Ibid., p. 236.
37. Ibid., p. 255.
38. Ibid.
39. Ibid., pp. 255–56.
40. See, for example, Bob Edwards and Michael W. Foley, "Social Capital and the Political Economy of Our Discontent," *American Behavioral Scientist,*

March/April 1997: 669–78; and Persell, "Interdependence."
41. Jeffrey C. Goldfarb, *The Cynical Society: The Culture of Politics and the Politics of Culture in American Life* (Chicago: University of Chicago, 1991), p. 18.
42. Emile Durkheim, *Suicide* (New York: Free Press, 1966), p. 252.
43. Ibid.
44. Bellah, *Emile Durkheim,* p. 146.
45. Durkheim, *Suicide,* p. 287.
46. A major reason for this disharmony is due to positions and relationships within the social order being based on "external" inequalities. I will discuss this more fully in Chapter 7, but briefly this means that factors such as race, gender, family name, and so on are more important for placement in the social structure than are "internal" inequalities, such as differences in ability, skill, and the like.
47. Bellah, *Emile Durkheim,* p. 191.
48. Goldfarb, *The Cynical Society.*

Chapter 6

1. Doug Podolsky and Betsy Streisand, "The Price of Vanity," *U.S. News and World Report,* October 14, 1996: 74–78.
2. Kathryn Pauly Morgan, "Women and the Knife," in R. Weitz (ed.), *The Politics of Women's Bodies: Sexuality, Appearance, and Behavior* (New York: Oxford, 1998), pp. 147–66.
3. Kathy Davis, "The Rise of the Surgical Fix," in K. Charmaz and D. A. Paterniti (eds.), *Health, Illness, and Healing: Society, Social Context, and Self* (Los Angeles: Roxbury, 1999), pp. 302–21.
4. Sharlene Hesse-Biber, *Am I Thin Enough: The Cult of Thinness and the Commercialization of Identity* (New York: Oxford, 1996).

5. The following descriptions on trends in beauty images are based on several sources: Hesse-Biber, *Am I Thin Enough;* Bridget Dolan and Inez Gitzinger, *Why Women? Gender Issues and Eating Disorders* (London: Athlone, 1994); April Fallon, "Culture in the Mirror: Sociocultural Determinants of Body Image," in T. F. Cash and T. Pruzinsky (eds.), *Body Images: Development, Deviance, and Change* (New York: Guilford, 1990), pp. 80–109; and Thomas Pruzinsky and Thomas F. Cash, "Integrative Themes in Body-Image Development, Deviance, and Change," in Cash and Pruzinsky, *Body Images,* pp. 337–349.

6. See, for example, Murray Webster, Jr. and James E. Driskell, Jr., "Beauty as Status," *American Journal of Sociology,* 1983: 140–65; K. K. Dion, E. Berscheid, and E. Walster, "What is Beautiful is Good," *Journal of Personality and Social Psychology,* 1972: 285–90; and Thomas F. Cash, "The Psychology of Physical Appearance: Aesthetics, Attributes, and Images," in Cash and Pruzinsky, *Body Images,* pp. 51–79.

7. Cash, "Psychology of Physical Appearance."

8. Hesse-Biber, *Am I Thin Enough.*

9. Arlie Russell Hochschild, *The Managed Heart: Commercialization of Human Feeling* (Berkeley: University of California, 1983), p. 7.

10. Ibid., p. 196.

11. Emile Durkheim, *The Elementary Forms of Religious Life* (New York: Free Press, 1965), p. 52.

12. Robert N. Bellah (ed.), *Emile Durkheim: On Morality and Society* (Chicago: University of Chicago, 1973), p. 159.

13. Ibid.

14. Catherine J. Garrett, "Recovery from Anorexia Nervosa: A Durkheimian Interpretation," *Social Science and Medicine,* 1996: 1489–1506.

15. Durkheim, *Elementary Forms of Religious Life,* p. 351.

16. Ibid., p. 345.

17. Ibid., p. 350.

18. Ibid., p. 356.

19. Ibid., p. 350.

20. Pirkko Markula, "Firm But Shapely, Fit But Sexy, Strong But Thin: The Postmodern Aerobicizing Female Bodies," *Sociology of Sport Journal,* 1995: 424–53.

21. Hesse-Biber, *Am I Thin Enough.*

22. See, for example, James C. Rosen, "Body-Image Disturbances in Eating Disorders," in Cash and Pruzinsky, *Body Images,* pp. 190–214; P. H. Collins, cited in K. S. Buchanan, "Creating Beauty in Blackness," in C. Brown and K. Jasper (eds.), *Consuming Passions: Feminist Approaches to Weight Preoccupation and Eating Disorders* (Toronto: Second Story Press, 1993), p. 79; and Hesse-Biber, *Am I Thin Enough.*

23. Paul Fussell, *Class* (New York: Summit, 1983).

24. Fallon, "Culture in the Mirror."

25. Karl Marx, *Capital,* vol. 1 (New York: International, 1977), p. 35.

26. The quote and income figures listed for baseball and football are drawn from Paul D. Staudohar, *Playing for Dollars: Labor Relations and the Sports Business* (Ithaca, NY: ILR Press, 1996), p. 2 and Chapters 2 and 3, respectively.

27. Ibid., p. 4.

28. George H. Sage, *Power and Ideology in American Sport* (Champaign, IL: Human Kinetics Books, 1990).

29. Joshua Gamson, *Claims to Fame: Celebrity in Contemporary America* (Berkeley: University of California, 1994), p. 45.

30. P. David Marshall, *Celebrity and Power: Fame in Contemporary Culture* (Minneapolis: University of Minnesota, 1997), p. 86.

31. Ibid., p. 189.

32. Ibid., p. 241.

33. Ibid., Ch. 5.

34. Catherine A. Steele and Kevin G. Barnhurst, "The Journalism of Opinion: Network News Coverage of U.S. Presidential Campaigns, 1968–1988," *Critical Studies in Mass Communication,* September 1996: 187–209.

35. This historical discussion relies heavily on the work of Staudohar, *Playing for Dollars;* Gamson, *Claims to Fame;* and Marshall, *Celebrity and Power.*

36. T. B. Bottomore and Maximilien Rubel (eds.), *Karl Marx: Selected Writings in Sociology and Social Philosophy* (New York: McGraw-Hill, 1964), pp. 51–52.

37. Gamson, *Claims to Fame,* p. 191.

38. Rogers Brubaker, *The Limits of Rationality* (London: George Allen & Unwin, 1984), p. 2.

39. Marshall, *Celebrity and Power,* p. 22.

40. Max Weber, *Economy and Society,* vol. 1 (New York: Bedminster, 1968), p. 241.

41. Ibid., vol. 3, p. 1122.

42. Ibid., p. 1135.

43. Marshall, *Celebrity and Power,* p. 55.

44. Max Weber, *The Methodology of the Social Sciences* (Glencoe, IL: Free Press, 1949), p. 53.

45. Weber, *Economy and Society,* vol. 1, p. 26.

46. The formulas and commentaries on the value of human life in this section are drawn from several sources: Michael Doan, "What a Life is Worth: U.S. Seeks a Price," *U.S. News & World Report,* September 16, 1985: 58; Daniel Seligman, "How Much Money is Your Life Worth?" *Fortune,* March 3, 1986: 25–27; "What a Life is Worth When One is Lost," *U.S. News & World Report,* February 27, 1989: 14–16; Dan R. Dalton and Richard A. Cosier, "An Issue of Corporate Social Responsibility: An Experiential Approach to Establish the Value of Human Life," *Journal of Business Ethics,* 1991: 311–315; and Steven Waldman, "Putting a Price Tag on Life," *Newsweek,* January 11, 1988: 40.

47. Quoted in Doan, "What a Life is Worth."

48. Margaret B. Carlson, "The Price of Life in Los Angeles," *Time,* February 22, 1988.

49. Gregory L. Weiss and Lynne E. Lonquist, *The Sociology of Health, Healing, and Illness* (Englewood Cliffs, NJ: Prentice-Hall, 1994), p. 187.

50. Daniel F. Chambliss, *Beyond Caring* (Chicago: University of Chicago, 1996), p. 41.

51. Frederic W. Hafferty, "Cadaver Stories and the Emotional Socialization of Medical Students," *Journal of Health and Social Behavior,* December 1988: 350 (italics mine).

52. Andrew Kimbrell, "The Body Enclosed: The Commodification of Human 'Parts,'" *The Ecologist,* July/August 1995: 134–41.

53. "Cloning: From Imagery to Ethics, 'Deeply Cool Stuff,'" *On Wisconsin,* March/April 1998: 28–29.

54. Jan Greene, "Has Managed Care Lost Its Soul?" *Hospitals & Health Networks,* May 20, 1997: 36–42. The quote is by James Sabin on p. 40.

55. Georg Simmel, *The Philosophy of Money* (Boston: Routledge, 1978), p. 232.

56. Ibid., p. 434.

57. Ibid., p. 235.

58. Ibid., p. 256.

Chapter 7

1. The discussion of Erik Wright's work on social class is drawn from Erik Olin Wright, "Class Boundaries in Advanced Capitalist Societies," *New Left Review,* vol. 98, 1976: 3–41; Erik Olin Wright, "Class Structure and Occupation: A Research Note," *Institute for Research on Poverty Discussion Paper No. 415-77* (Madison: University of Wisconsin, 1977); Erik Olin Wright and Donmoon Cho, "The Relative Permeability of Class Boundaries to Cross-Class Friendships: A Comparative Study of the United States, Canada, Sweden, and Norway," *American Sociological Review,* vol. 57, 1992: 85–102; and Mark Western and Erik Olin Wright, "The Permeability of Class Boundaries to Intergenerational Mobility among Men in the United States, Canada, Norway and Sweden," *American Sociological Review,* vol. 59, 1994: 606–29.

2. See, for example, Jared Bernstein and Lawrence Mishel, "Has Wage Inequality Stopped Growing?" *Monthly Labor Review,* December 1997: 3–16; Robert I. Lerman, "Reassessing Trends in U.S. Earnings Inequality," *Monthly Labor Review,* December 1997: 17–25; Peter Passell, "Blue Collar Loses Ground," *Akron Beacon Journal,* June 14, 1998: P1 and P14; and Tamar Lewin, "Wage Difference Between Women and Men Widens," *New York Times,* September 15, 1997: A1 and A8.

3. John Byrne, "How High Can CEO Pay Go?" *Business Week,* April 22, 1996: 100–106.

4. Marcy Gordon, "CEOs Still Rewarded for Big Layoffs," *Akron Beacon Journal,* May 2, 1997: D9 and D10.

5. Passell, "Blue Collar Loses Ground," p. A14.

6. U.S. Bureau of the Census, *Money Income in the United States: 1996,* Current Population Reports P60-197 (Washington, DC: U.S. Government Printing Office, 1997).

7. Robert Reich has recently suggested this bifurcation of the middle class. See his *The Work of Nations: Preparing Ourselves for 21st Century Capitalism* (New York: A. A. Knopf, 1991). The quotes are from Dennis Farney, "Elite Theory: Have Liberals Ignored 'Have-Less' Whites at Their Own Peril?" *Wall Street Journal,* December 14, 1994: A1; see also John Dillin, "U.S. Could Lose Middle Class," *Christian Science Monitor,* June 18, 1991: 6.

8. Timothy Egan, "The Rich are Different: They Can Afford Homes," *New York Times,* November 16, 1994: A8.

9. U.S. Bureau of the Census, *Asset Ownership of Households: 1993.* [Online]. Available at www.census.gov/ftp/pub/hhes/wealth/wlth93f.html; Sylvia Nasar, "The Rich Get Richer, But Never the Same Way Twice," *New York Times,* August 16, 1992: E3; Edward N. Wolff, "Changing Inequality of Wealth," *American Economic Review,* May 1992: 552–58; and Edward N. Wolff, "How the Pie is Sliced," *The American Prospect,* vol. 22, 1995: 58–64.

10. Thomas R. Dye, *Who's Running America? The Clinton Years* (Englewood Cliffs, NJ: Prentice-Hall, 1995), pp. 15ff. Quote from p. 23.

11. See, for example, Frank Levy and Richard J. Murnane, "U.S. Earnings Levels and Earnings Inequality: A Review of Recent Trends and Proposed Explanations," *Journal of Economic Literature,* vol. 30, 1992: 1333–81; William Hershey, "Temporary Workers Growing in Numbers," *Akron Beacon Journal,* June 16, 1993: B7; W.

Norton Grubb and Robert H. Wilson, "Trends in Wage and Salary Inequality, 1967–88," *Monthly Labor Review,* June 1992: 23–39; and U.S. Bureau of the Census, *Workers with Low Earnings: 1964 to 1990,* Current Population Reports, P60-178 (Washington, DC: U.S. Government Printing Office, 1992).

12. T. B. Bottomore and Maximilien Rubel (eds.), *Karl Marx: Selected Writings in Sociology and Social Philosophy* (New York: McGraw-Hill, 1964), p. 178.

13. Karl Marx, *Capital,* vol. 1 (New York: International, 1967), p. 349.

14. Ibid., p. 360.

15. See, for example, the classic studies by Robert Blauner, *Alienation and Freedom* (Chicago: University of Chicago, 1964); and Melvin L. Kohn, "Occupational Structure and Alienation," *American Journal of Sociology,* vol. 82, 1976: 111–30.

16. Ruth Milkman, *Farewell to the Factory: Auto Workers in the Late Twentieth Century* (Berkeley: University of California, 1997), p. 13.

17. Katherine S. Newman, *Falling From Grace* (New York: Vintage, 1988), p. 200.

18. Marx, *Capital,* vol. 1, p. 763.

19. Beth A. Rubin, "Class Struggle American Style: Unions, Strikes and Wages," *American Sociological Review,* vol. 51, 1986: 618–31.

20. These quotes are from Simmel are in Nicholas J. Spykman, *The Social Theory of Georg Simmel* (New York: Atherton, 1966), p. 188.

21. These quotes are from Georg Simmel, *The Philosophy of Money* (Boston: Routledge, 1978), pp. 210–18.

22. Spykman, *Georg Simmel,* p. 189.

23. U.S. Bureau of the Census, *Asset Ownership of Households: 1993.*

24. U.S. Bureau of the Census, *Money Income in the United States;* U.S. Bureau of the Census, *Poverty in the United States: 1996,* Current Population Reports P60-198 (Washington, DC: U.S. Government Printing Office, 1997).

25. Heidi Hartmann, quoted in Tamar Lewin, "Wage Difference Between Women and Men Widens," *New York Times,* September 15, 1997: A8.

26. The income, poverty, wealth, occupational, and earnings differences between racial and gender groups are drawn from several sources: U.S. Bureau of the Census, *Money Income in the United States: 1996* (Washington, DC: U.S. Government Printing Office, September 1997); U.S. Bureau of the Census, *Poverty in the United States: 1996* (Washington, DC: U.S. Government Printing Office, September 1997); U.S. Bureau of the Census, *Income, Poverty, and Valuation of Noncash Benefits: 1994* (Washington, DC: U.S. Government Printing Office, April 1996); U.S. Bureau of the Census, *Asset Ownership of Households: 1993;* U.S. Department of Labor, *Employment and Earnings* (Washington, DC: U.S Government Printing Office, January 1996); Marcia L. Bellas, "Comparable Worth in Academia: The Effects of Faculty Salaries of the Sex Composition and Labor-Market Conditions of Academic Disciplines," *American Sociological Review,* vol. 59, 1994: 807–21.

27. Stanley Feldstein (ed.), *The Poisoned Tongue: A Documentary History of American Racism and Prejudice* (New York: William Morrow, 1972), p. 13.

28. Martin N. Marger, *Race and Ethnic Relations: American and Global Perspectives* (Belmont, CA: Wadsworth, 1997).

29. Cecilia L. Ridgeway, Elizabeth Heger Boyle, Kathy J. Kuipers, and Dawn T. Robinson, "How Do Status Beliefs Develop? The Role of Resources and Interactional Experience," *American Sociological Review,* vol. 63, 1998: 331–50.

30. H. H. Gerth and C. Wright Mills, *From Max Weber* (New York: Oxford, 1962), p. 190.

31. James E. Blackwell, *The Black Community: Diversity and Unity* (New York: Harper & Row, 1985); Stanley Elkins, *Slavery: A Problem in American Institutional and Intellectual Life* (Chicago: University of Chicago, 1959); John Hope Franklin, *From Slavery to Freedom: A History of Negro Americans* (New York: A. A. Knopf, 1980); and George M. Frederickson, *White Supremacy: A Comparative Study in American and South African History* (New York: Oxford, 1981). On the effects of disenfranchisement, see Pamela Barnhouse Walters, David R. James, and Holly J. McCammon, "Citizenship and Public Schools: Accounting for Racial Inequality in Education in the Pre- and Post-Disenfranchisement South," *American Sociological Review,* vol. 62, 1997: 34–52.

32. Emile Durkheim, *The Division of Labor* (New York: Free Press, 1933), p. 353.

33. Ibid.

34. Ibid., pp. 354, 368.

35. Ibid., p. 374.

36. Ibid., p. 375.

A Summing Up

1. Edward O. Wilson, "The Biological Basis of Morality," *Atlantic Monthly,* April 1998: 53–70.

2. Kenneth Brower, "Photography in the Age of Falsification," *Atlantic Monthly,* May 1998: 92–111.